KT-871-398

Contents

Country Distinguishing Signs

On some maps, international distinguishing signs have been used to indicate the location of countries which surround Austria. Thus:

H = Hungary
SK = Slovakia

This book employs a simple rating system to help choose which places to visit:

✓	'top ten'

♦♦♦   do not miss
♦♦   see if you can
♦   worth seeing if you have time

INTRODUCTION

Tucked into the northeastern corner of Austria, Vienna has long been the crossroads of Europe, where east meets west and Hungarian goulash, Turkish coffee and old-world courtesies are all 'local' institutions. For 600 years, the Habsburgs held court here, received deputations from the furthest corners of the Holy Roman Empire, swallowed up their

On the edge of the old town, the Burgtheater is centre stage in the German-speaking world

neighbours, and fought off invasions which all too often beat right on the doors of the capital. Amid all the warring and diplomatic intrigue, the Viennese created an immensely cultured and leisurely lifestyle which has remained part of the city's great attraction.

Whipped cream and waltzes represent two bastions of Viennese social life. The heavenly coffee houses and *Konditoreien* (pastry shops) are where you will find whipped cream with everything and where you cannot conceivably escape without at least 2,000 calories on board. Johann Strauss' *Tales from the Vienna Woods* and *The Blue Danube* personify the lighthearted gaiety of Vienna's glittering palace balls, particularly the Christmas season, accompanied by early snowfalls and Christmas markets. A third bastion is the flourishing music scene. This is the home of Mozart, Beethoven, Haydn, Schubert, Brahms, Bruckner, Mahler – the list goes on, and the Viennese are proud of it. In fact, 'smug' would be a more appropriate description if they didn't enjoy it so much. (There are concerts galore in the summer season, but do book ahead for special events and the Vienna Boys' Choir to avoid disappointment.)

In addition to all the goings-on, there is the setting. According to Lady Mary Wortley Montagu in 1716: 'It is very large and almost wholly composed of delicious Palaces'. Vienna may not seem so large today, but those 'delicious Palaces' are still a treat: Prince Eugene's Belvedere; Maria Theresa's favourite, the Schönbrunn; and the imposing, if not exactly edible, Hofburg, are the most stately. The old city (Innere Stadt) is girdled by Emperor Franz Josef's 19th-century Ringstrasse, which boasts a host of slightly less grand palaces built for the nobility; and an excursion to Dürnstein will reveal the ruins of a 12th-century castle where Richard the Lionheart was imprisoned by Duke Leopold V. On top of the calorific pastries, there is no shortage of other foods in Vienna. Austrian portion control is generous to the point of leaving you quite unable to get up from the table. There are two types of traditional drinking establishments worth investigating, and you can usually eat at them, too. The first is the *Beisl*, a sort of comfortable old-world tavern where you can kick the snow off your boots and defrost, or escape the summer heat. The other option is a *Heuriger*, which sells refreshing young wines from local vineyards. There are several in town, but the most authentic are found out in the suburbs set amongst the vineyards themselves.

In this guide, you will find an honest sampling of the best that is on offer, and how to avoid the pitfalls.

The elegant 18th-century Gloriette colonnade stands in the grounds of the palace of Schönbrunn

BACKGROUND

The Romans called it *Vindobona* when they
arrived in the 1st century AD, moved on the
Celts, and set up a garrison in what is now the
Innere Stadt. They had come from Britain under
the leadership of Emperor Marcus Aurelius to
defend the Roman Empire's eastern
boundaries. It was thanks to a subsequent
emperor, Probus, that the first vines were
introduced on the slopes of the Wienerwald.
After the Romans, Vienna was overrun by

Goths, Bavarians, Magyars and more, until the 10th century, when the Margraves of Babenberg succeeded in driving the Magyars out and settled down to create a stable independent state on the Danube trade route. To honour their achievement the Holy Roman Empire made the Babenbergs hereditary Dukes of Austria in 1156.

During the Middle Ages, Austria prospered, generating the first Golden Age of Vienna. The original Romanesque St Stephen's was built, and so were St Ruprecht's and St Peter's. Trade, the arts and crafts all flourished, attracting immigrant merchants and artisans. Because of its location, Vienna became an obvious stop for the Crusaders *en route* to Jerusalem. In the 13th century, a further construction boom saw the building of the Michaelerkirche, along with monasteries and noble mansions in what has become the Innere Stadt. Trade flourished further and minstrel music was heard in the elegant new residences. When the Babenberg line died out, Ottokar II of Bohemia took up the reins, proving popular with the locals, who sided with him against the attempts of the new German King Rudolf von Habsburg to take control of the city in 1276. Two years later, Rudolf occupied Vienna and initiated a period of Habsburg rule that was to last until 1918.

The Habsburgs

The Habsburgs were a German family who could trace their lineage back to 10th-century Alsace, and had taken their name from one of their own castles, Habichtsburg or Falcon's Castle. The rulers were many and varied, some out to build empires, others preferring to build at home.

Maximilian I, Karl V and Ferdinand I were among those to neglect Vienna, while Rudolf IV, 'The Founder', endowed the university in 1365 and began to rebuild St Stephen's in the Gothic style. Friedrich III finished the work, was elected Holy Roman Emperor in 1452, and won Rome's approval to elevate Vienna to the status of a bishopric in 1469. By the end of the 15th century, Austria had become one of the major players on the European stage, securing its

Known as the Steffl, the Stephansdom South Tower rises to 450 feet (137m)

position with a series of advantageous marriages which led to Hungarian King Matthias Corvinus' famous remark: 'Let others wage war, while you, happy Austria, arrange marriages. What Mars gives to others, you receive from Venus'. For instance, Maximilian I's marriage to Maria of Burgundy added the Low Countries, and then Burgundy after the Battle of Nancy. His son Philip's marriage added Spain. The double wedding of Maximilian's grandchildren, Ferdinand and Maria, brought the addition of Hungary and Bohemia.

BACKGROUND

The Austrians did not have it all their own way.
In 1529, Vienna was under siege from the
Turkish Suleiman, a campaign which did not
quite succeed, but did introduce coffee. A
revolt in Bohemia opened the Thirty Years War,
resulting in a Swedish occupation in parts of
Austria; and the Turks returned in 1683, only to
be driven back to the Balkans in a campaign
that made Prince Eugene of Savoy a hero. The
great general celebrated his victory by
commissioning former fortress builder Johann

Lukas von Hildebrandt to design the magnificent Belvedere Palace. It was the age of baroque, and Vienna was transformed into one vast salon, a magnetic attraction for musicians, artists and roaming royalty looking for entertainment. When not erecting imposing monuments, civic buildings and churches, architects like von Hildebrandt, Johann Bernhard Fischer von Erlach and his son, Joseph Emanuel, designed grandiose palaces. The Schwarzenbergs, Auersbergs and Liechtensteins all found the money to build them. Karl VI tried to recreate the Escorial at Klosterneuburg; the Karlskirche was designed to emulate St Peter's in Rome; while the Schönbrunn was expanded on a grand scale to rival Versailles.

Amid all this, along came Empress Maria Theresa, who ascended the throne in 1740. She was kind, pious, caring of her people and the mother of 16 children, who created the imperial apothecary, where palace servants could obtain free medical service, and introduced vaccinations against smallpox. She was a good seamstress and loved to sing. Indeed, she loved music of all kinds and often commanded operas and concerts to be performed at the Schönbrunn Palace, a summer home she much preferred to the grim Hofburg. Her orchestra director was Christoph Gluck (the father of modern opera), while a young Joseph Haydn sang in the Vienna Boys' Choir. Together with her husband, Franz Stefan of Lorraine, Maria Theresa guided the Empire through three wars (with the loss of Silesia), reformed taxation and administration, bolstered the Imperial coffers and arranged diplomatic marriages for all her children save the favourite, Marie-Christine.

Maria Theresa was brought to the throne by the War of Austrian Succession

Maria Theresa's son, Joseph II, succeeded her in 1780, and pushed through a series of radical social reforms which thoroughly upset the conservative local populace. They were happier with Joseph's nephew, Franz II, who transformed Austria into a police state in order to combat any revolutionary repercussions in the wake of events in France (where Maria Theresa's daughter, Marie Antoinette, lost her head).

BACKGROUND

The French Occupation

In 1804, Franz II became Franz I when he ceded the title of Holy Roman Emperor and emerged as Emperor Franz I of Austria. Meanwhile, the 'Corsican' was on the move; the French army occupied Vienna in 1805, and Napoleon installed himself at Schönbrunn. When the French returned in 1809, Emperor Franz decided to save what was left of his empire by marrying his daughter, Marie-Louise, to Napoleon in 1810.

The downfall of Napoleon put Vienna back on the map with the glittering Congress of Vienna in 1815. Franz's capable Chancellor, Prince Metternich, handled the serious business of slicing up Napoleon's Europe, while the Emperor himself organised balls and concerts to entertain the likes of Wellington and the Tsar of Russia. Contemporary cynics dubbed it the congress that 'dances but does not move'. After the congress, Vienna enjoyed 30 peaceful

The Kunsthistorisches Museum is a treasure house of fine art

Vienna's musical pedigree is superb and includes Mozart, Haydn, the Strausses and Mahler

years of *Backhendlzeit* (the roast chicken era), one of good living, more music and dancing, when Beethoven won favour and Johann Strauss (father and son) pioneered the waltz. Revolution did come to Vienna, briefly, in 1848. Metternich was forced to resign, and Franz's successor, the totally unsatisfactory Ferdinand, abdicated in favour of his 18-year-old nephew, the earnest and soldierly Franz Josef. Still referred to by Austrians as the 'Old Gentleman', Franz Josef ruled for 68 years, during which time his foreign policy was largely disastrous, but Vienna benefited enormously. His vision of a great European capital city generated the Ringstrasse, with its elegant residences, which set the standard for half a century of Viennese building activity. He brought marble from around the world to construct the Kunsthistorisches Museum; added the Burgtheater, Opera House, and Town Hall; and created a romantic legend with his marriage to Elisabeth of Bovaria in 1854. Beautiful, talented and spirited, an expert horsewoman and keep-fit fanatic, Empress 'Sisi' found court life too constraining. She was often absent, and after the suicide of her son, Crown Prince Rudolf, in 1889, she roamed around Europe until she was assassinated in Geneva in 1898.

The Universal Exhibition of 1873

The last great flourish of Habsburg accomplishment was the 1873 World Fair, when the city's grand new Staatsoper, theatres, concert halls and museums drew an audience from across Europe to admire the imposing buildings and the music of Brahms, Bruckner, Mahler, Lehar and Strauss. But it was the end of an era. Franz Josef's heir, Archduke Franz Ferdinand, was assassinated in Sarajevo, an event which precipitated World War I. He was succeeded by his grand nephew, Karl I, whose two short years of rule were spent presiding over the dissolution of the Austro-Hungarian Empire. In 1918, Karl was forced to sign away the empire and its powers (though not its crown) and flee with his wife from Schönbrunn to his private shooting lodge.

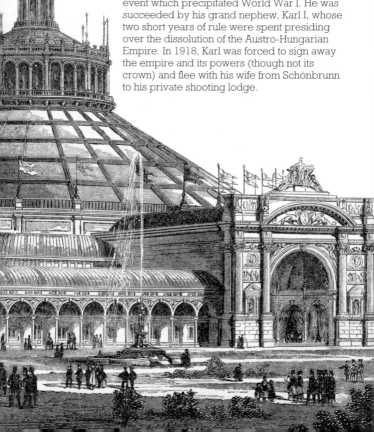

A New Republic

Following the Empire's defeat and dissolution after World War I, Austria's new republican government sought union with Germany (Anschluss). The peace treaty of Saint Germain forbade Anschluss and imposed war reparations. The country was thrown into economic and political turmoil, and in 1933 the Austrian Parliament was suspended. A year later, the Austrian nationalist Chancellor Dollfuss was killed in a failed Nazi coup. It was only a matter of time before Hitler, as he had promised in his autobiography *Mein Kampf*, imposed Anschluss by annexing Austria in 1938. After World War II Austria was liberated by the Allies. Vienna and the rest of the country was divided between the four powers (the Soviet Union, the US, Britain and France). With the help of Marshall Aid, the Austrians rebuilt their economy. In 1955 the Second Republic finally gained sovereign status as a democratic, federal and neutral state, with a President as ceremonial head of state and Chancellor as head of government.

For most of the post-war period economic growth was matched by political stability. However, in the late 1970s a less stable period followed in the wake of economic scandals. The election of Kurt Waldheim as President in 1986 led to bitter controversy about his role in the War. Sinowatz, the Socialist Chancellor, resigned in protest at Waldheim's election. In the general election a few months later there was a dramatic increase in the right-wing nationalist vote, the environmentalist Green Party entered the National Assembly for the first time and the coalition of the Socialist Party and People's Party, first seen during the Allied occupation, re-emerged as the governing force. Austria joined the EU in 1995.

Today Vienna is a prosperous city, home to 20 per cent of Austria's population. The city's Habsburg edifices give it an air of aristocratic indifference, and travellers who are operating on a tight budget will find that it can be an expensive place to stay; but the packed coffee houses off the Opernring and the Prater's buzzing fairground show the spirit of the city is still very much alive.

WHAT TO SEE

For sightseeing purposes, Vienna can be divided, quite naturally, into two distinct parts. The Innere Stadt (Inner City) comprises the Old Town, bordered by the Danube and encircled by the Habsburgs' monumental Ringstrasse (which follows the foundations of the original city walls). Clustered around the Stephansdom, this is an area of medieval back alleys, baroque churches, noble palaces and pedestrianised zones – a jumble of the past with the largest concentration of tourist sights. Since few buses operate within the First District (one of 23) it is best seen on foot. Another alternative is to be as romantic as the Viennese themselves and take to the *Fiaker* (the two-horse open carriage which has been in existence since the 17th century) with its bowler-hatted driver, who will gladly show you the sights, at a price.

There is also much of interest beyond the confines of Ringstrasse in the outlying districts collectively known as the 'Vorstadt'. Walking through them is the best way to come into contact with ordinary Viennese city life as well as some of the city's most spectacular sights.

Information on opening times etc has been provided for guidance only. We have tried to ensure accuracy, but things do change and we would advise readers to check locally before planning visits to avoid any possible disappointment.

Vienna's Rathaus at night

Inner City Attractions

AKADEMIE DER BILDENDEN KÜNSTE
Schillerplatz 3
Well worth a visit, Vienna's Academy of Fine Arts boasts one of the finest galleries of Old Masters in a German-speaking country. One of the highlights on display here is Hieronymus Bosch's *The Last Judgement*. There is also an excellent Venetian series by Guardi, as well as works by Cranach the Elder, Dirk Bouts, Van Dyck and Rembrandt.
Open: Tuesday, Thursday, Friday 10.00–14.00 hrs, Wednesday 10.00–13.00 hrs and 15.00–18.00 hrs, weekend 09.00–13.00 hrs.

Guided Walks
A variety of specialised guided walks can be made of the city, from one which looks at links to the film, *The Third Man*, to one which explores Sigmund Freud's connections with Vienna. Information is available from Wiener Tourismusverband, Obere Augartenstrasse 40 (tel: 211 140). (See also **Tours** in the **Directory**, page 123).

WHAT TO SEE

ALBERTINA
Augustinerstrasse 1
Housed at the southern end of the Hofburg, the Albertina State Collection of Graphic Art comprises around 40,000 drawings and over a million prints. There are superb examples of miniature painting and book illustrations, historically valuable architectural plans and political cartoons. The collection includes works from 15th-century Dutch, German and Italian masters right through to contemporary times, and features such great talents as Leonardo da Vinci, Michelangelo, Raphael, Dürer, Rubens, Rembrandt, Canaletto and Fragonard.
Closed for renovation until 1999.

ALTE SCHMIEDE
Schönlaterngasse 9
A chance to revisit a bygone era when horse-power ruled and old smithies such as this kept the world going round. Nowadays the cellar houses a museum of wrought iron.
Open: Monday to Friday 10.00–15.00 hrs.

ALTES RATHAUS
Wipplingerstrasse 8
In 1316, Duke Friedrich the Fair gave this house (confiscated from a rebellious citizen) to the town. It served as the town hall until a new building was erected on the Ring. Behind the handsome 17th-century façade, a courtyard features the famous Andromeda Fountain by Donner.
Open: Monday, Wednesday, Thursday 09.00–17.00hrs.

ALTE UNIVERSITÄT
Bäckerstrasse
Franz Schubert once lived here (the Old University) when he was a member of the Vienna Boy's Choir. Founded in 1365, it was closed down after an 1848 student revolution, when the authorities retaliated by moving the protestors to academies in outlying districts until a new university was built on the Ring in 1884. The building is now the Academy of Sciences.

ANKERUHR
Hoher Markt 10
One of Vienna's favourite curiosities, the Anker clock, is set into an archway across Rotgasse, facing onto Hoher Markt. Donated to 'the people of Vienna' by the local Anker Insurance Company in 1912, Franz Matsch's colourful, animated clock illustrates the story of Vienna in 12 parts. Various historical figures edge across the clock face each hour, and at noon you can see the whole parade from Roman Emperor Marcus Aurelius through dukes, counts, kings and emperors to Joseph Haydn – the only musician on the bill.

AUGUSTINERKIRCHE
Augustinerstrasse 7 (off Josefsplatz)
Originally attached to a monastery founded by Friedrich the Fair in 1327, St Augustine's Church was a favourite with Vienna's 'First Family', the Habsburgs, when it came to staging a momentous event. It was here, for instance, that

Maria Theresa married Franz Stefan of Lorraine in 1736, thus securing her rights to the Empire. Though Napoleon wasn't exactly present, the church witnessed his marriage

Anker clock: time for history

in absentia to the unfortunate Marie-Louise in 1810, and the full-blown nuptials of Franz Josef and Elisabeth of Bavaria in 1854.

WHAT TO SEE

The Vienna Boy's Choir

Many Habsburgs are also buried behind the Gothic exterior. One of the most famous graves is that of Archduchess Marie-Christine while the Herzgrüfterl houses a line-up of silver urns containing the hearts of 54 Habsburgs. If you enjoy superb church music, this is one of the best places to hear it.

BÄCKERSTRASSE

You will find Vienna's old 'street of the bakers' lined with 16th- and 17th-century houses, now mainly occupied by antique dealers and art galleries. Among the sights, No 7 fronts a lovely Renaissance courtyard (one of the few remaining in the city), opposite the former home of Madame de Staël; there is the 1627 baroque-style Church of the Assumption just off the street; and a baroque house at No 16 which was once a famous restaurant serving students cheap meals concocted of leftovers from the Hofburg kitchens.

BALLHAUSPLATZ

More important historically than architecturally, No 2 Ballhausplatz is the refined 18th-century Office of the Austrian Federal Chancellor. Early Chancellors lived there too, such as Count (later Prince) Metternich who held the reins from 1809 until the 1848 revolution, when he was forced into exile to England. Metternich and his successors plotted the shape of Europe from behind these walls; Chancellor Dollfuss was assassinated by the Nazis here in 1934; and Federal President Miklas received Hitler's ultimatum before the 1938 invasion of Austria.

◆

BEETHOVEN-ERINNERUNGSRÄUME
Pasqualatihaus, Mölkerbastei 8
The Memorial Rooms are housed in one of the composer's several Vienna homes, this one built for an admirer of his work, a Herr Pasqualati, in 1797. Beethoven lived here on and off between 1804 and 1815, during which time he composed the *Leonora Overtures* and the Third Symphony, the *Eroica*. Memorabilia on view includes a lock of his hair, the type of piano he used to play and a facsimile of part of *Fidelio*, the opera score he also worked on while living here.
Open: Tuesday to Sunday 09.00–12.15 hrs and 13.00–16.30 hrs.

◆◆

BUNDESMOBILIENSAMMLUNG
Mariahilfer Strasse 88
If you are intrigued by the Imperial family, you will certainly want to visit the former Court Furniture Repository, and check out the eclectic selection of period furniture and household items which once belonged to them. A fascinating insight into a bygone age with plenty of artistic and historic merit on display. There are

guided tours on the hour.
Open: Tuesday to Friday 09.00–16.00 hrs, Saturday 09.00–12.00 hrs.

BURGKAPELLE
Hofburg, Schweizerhof
The Castle Chapel is home to the world-famous Vienna Boys' Choir, and lies at the heart of the Hofburg in a niche off the Schweizerhof. The Gothic-style building was founded by Emperor Ferdinand III, and completed in 1449. Later, it had a baroque overhaul, but was partly restored to its original design in 1802. The very first Boys' Choir accompanied church services for the Court under the patronage of Maximilian I as far back as 1498. With just one brief hiatus between 1918 and 1924, the choir has notched up almost 500 years of continuous excellence, with its Golden Age in the 17th and 18th centuries, inspired by the works of Beethoven, Mozart and Haydn (the latter was a child chorister, as was Franz Schubert). Today, there are four working choirs of 24 boys each operating under the mantle of the Vienna Boys' Choir. At any one time, two are on tour; a third rests; while the fourth conducts a sung Mass on Sundays and Holy Days from January to mid June and mid September to December at 09.15 hrs. Seats must be reserved well in advance, although there is limited free standing room. Written orders can be sent to: Hofmusikkapelle, Hofburg, A-1010 Vienna. Guided tours depart mid-January to June and

mid-September to mid-December on Tuesday and Thursday at 14.30, 14.45, 15.00, 15.15 and 15.30 hrs.

BURGTHEATER
Dr Karl-Lueger-Ring 2
If you are a German-speaking theatre lover, who has managed to acquire a much sought-after ticket, this is bordering on a four-star attraction. Vienna's leading theatre, the 19th-century Burgtheater is considered one of the finest in the German-speaking world, and whether or not you succeed in securing a ticket for a performance here, a guided tour is well-worth your time. Refurbished after fire damage in the 1950s, there are frescos by the Klimt brothers crowning the staircase, and the foyer is hung with portraits of famous actors. Tours depart July and August Monday to Saturday at 13.00, 14.00 and 15.00 hrs; April to June, September and October, Tuesday and Thursday at 16.00 hrs, Sunday 15.00 hrs.

DEUTSCHORDENSKIRCHE
Singerstrasse 7
A grand 14th-century Gothic church with baroque additions, this was the spiritual home of the former Order of Teutonic Knights. Led by the Holy Roman Emperor of the German nation (usually a Habsburg), this military order was active in the Baltic area during the Middle Ages, and the church is decorated with memorabilia including banners and shields, plus a superb 16th-century triptych from Mechelen. Their valuable Treasury

(Schatzkammer des Deutschen Ordens) containing finely-wrought ornaments and table-ware, coins, medals, jewellery, portraits and documents is displayed in a suite of rooms above the church.
Open: May to October Monday, Thursday, weekend 10.00–12.00 hrs and Wednesday, Friday, Saturday 15.00–17.00 hrs; November to April Monday, Thursday, Saturday 10.00–12.00 hrs, Wednesday, Friday, Saturday 15.00–17.00 hrs.

◆◆
FAHNRICHSHOF
corner of Blutgasse and Singerstrasse
An attractive complex of artists studios, galleries and boutiques intermingled with apartments and gardens that illustrate the finer points of urban renovation.

◆◆
FIGAROHAUS
Domgasse 5
Wolfgang Amadeus Mozart's home from 1784 to 1787, during one of the happiest and most prolific periods of his life. While the composer lived here with his wife and son, he composed several concertos, quintets, trios, sonatas and the opera *The Marriage of Figaro*, from which the house takes its name. Mozart was appointed Chamber Composer to the Imperial Court, which attracted a number of famous pupils and visitors such as Beethoven, Haydn and Hummel. The memorial rooms in the Figarohaus contain memorabilia, including the first German language libretto of *The Marriage of Figaro*. The composer's work room boasts a

fine stucco ceiling commissioned by a previous tenant, Albert Camesina. (The house was formerly called *Camesinahaus*, and the front entrance was on Schulergasse.) *Open*: Tuesday to Sunday 09.00– 12.15 hrs and 13.00–14.30 hrs.

◆
FINANZMINISTERIUM
Himmelpfortgasse 3
Formerly Prince Eugene's winter palace, the 18th-century Finance Ministry was designed

by J B Fischer von Erlach. Its much decorated façade is typical of his early work. Visitors are permitted to view the vestibule and magnificent ceremonial staircase by Giovanni Giuliani. A series of rooms (the gold cabinet) survives from the 18th century and has been restored.

◆
FLEISCHMARKT
A narrow little street that used to be the meat market from way back in 1285 until the 19th century. Before 1200, the street was part of the medieval

In the limelight: the Burgtheater

commercial suburb outside the city walls.

Where Fleischmarkt meets Griechengasse, you will find the ivy-swagged Griechenbeisl (Greeks' Tavern) at No 22, a café once haunted by musical types like Beethoven, Schubert and Strauss, and where Mark Twain wrote *The Million Pound Note*.

◆
FRANZISKANERPLATZ
Make a quick stop in this little square to admire the

Freyung and the Schottenkirche

18th-century fountain adorned with a statue of *Moses* by Johann Martin Fischer, and set against the ornately baroque background of the Franziskanerkirche.

The latter church is a particularly interesting architectural mix of southern German Renaissance and Gothic features. Inside, its key features are a splendid *trompe l'oeil* high altar and a 1642 organ.

◆◆
FREYUNG

Called a square but actually a triangle, the Freyung is bordered by the diminutive Palais Harrach on one side (where Haydn's mother was once family cook), and the Schottenkirche (Church of the Scots) on the other. Originally founded by Celtic monks in the 12th century, the present church actually dates from the 17th century. The monks, who were in fact Irish, not Scottish, arrived in Austria at the invitation of Duke Heinrich II 'Jasomirgott', a pious type who earned his nickname from a much-repeated catchphrase 'Ja, so mir Gott helfe' (Yes, if God will help me). A modern monument in his honour stands to one side of the church. The Scottish Madonna is Vienna's earliest statue of Mary and there are some fine tombs in the crypt, including that of Duke Heinrich. In the middle of Freyung, the Austria Fountain is decorated with allegorical figures representing the various rivers within the country. To the south lies one of the Inner City's major arteries, Herrengasse, an aristocratic street flanked by column-fronted town houses and palaces that have since become government ministries.

◆◆
GRABEN

A not-to-be-missed fashionable shopping street these days, Graben follows the line of the ancient 'graben' (ditch) which once formed the southern

Once a Roman defensive ditch, Graben is now a popular stamping ground for shoppers

WHAT TO SEE

boundary of the Roman military camp.

Later it was famous for its coffee houses and also for being an infamous red light district where the 'Graben nymphs' (as the prostitutes were called) sold their favours.

Nowadays, broad Graben is altogether different, more chic,

Pedestrianised Graben in the shadow of the shops

and pedestrianised, dominated by a rather strange landmark, the Pestsäule (Pillar of the Plague), which was erected in gratitude for Vienna's deliverance from the plague, which had struck the city in 1679.

◆
HAUS DER GESELLSCHAFT DER MUSIKFREUNDE
Bösendorferstrasse 12
In this section of the Musikverein, home of the Vienna Philharmonic Orchestra, dedicated music *aficionados* can pore over original manuscripts by Beethoven, Mozart, Schubert, Haydn, Bruckner and many others amassed by the Gesellschaft der Musikfreunde (Music Lovers' Society).
Open: October to June Monday, Wednesday, Friday 09.00–13.00 hrs or by appointment.

HOFBURG ✓

Michaelerplatz
If there is any one place to visit in Vienna, then the Hofburg has to be it. It was, after all the official residence of the Habsburg rulers for 600 years, from the 13th century until 1918, and sprawls across 47 acres of the southwest corner of the Inner City in a confusing jumble of buildings which run the gamut of architectural styles from Gothic to rococo. From simple beginnings as a 13th-century keep, the Hofburg grew

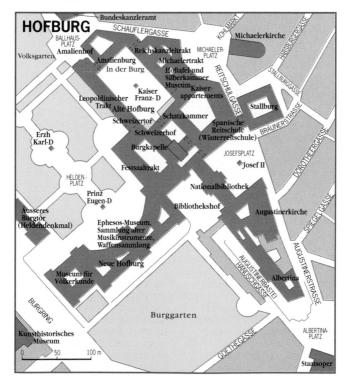

WHAT TO SEE

on a colossal scale, and although half the complex is used for governmental purposes these days, that still leaves plenty of room for several museums and collections, the National Library, the Treasury, the Spanish Riding School and a couple of churches. They can all be visited separately, and are included in these listings under individual headings. In the whole of the Hofburg complex there are some 2,600 rooms. The oldest sections are the Schweizerhof, Burgkapelle and Palais Amalienburg, which span the period up to the early 17th century.

The next great stage of development was the construction of the Leopoldinischer Trakt, commissioned by Leopold I in 1660 to link the Schweizerhof and Amalienburg, and as part of his master plan to build a fabulous Habsburg palace to rival that of Louis XIV at Versailles. The baroque façade now conceals the Austrian President's office. Across the courtyard, J E Fischer von Erlach's Reichskanzlei, (Imperial Chancellery) shares the baroque motif, and contains Franz Josef's apartments. The emperor gave the go-ahead for the Michaelerplatz wing (backing on to the Reichskanzlei), the Neue Hofburg, and plans were drawn up for an Emperors' Forum covering the old parade ground. It would have encompassed Heldenplatz (Heroes' Square), but was never completed, although work continued on the Neue Hofburg until the 1920s, after the Empire had crumbled.

HOFTAFEL UND SILBERKAMMER MUSEUM

Hofburg Michaelerplatz
Reopened in 1995 after renovation, this is a priceless collection of Imperial tableware and silver cutlery from Europe and the Far East, accrued over the centuries by generations of Habsburgs on wedding days and birthdays. Anyone who admires fine glassware and porcelain cannot fail to fall in love with these royal items and wish perhaps they owned a table large enough to accommodate the 140-piece Meissen dinner service or the neo-Renaissance centrepiece bestowed on Franz Josef by Britain's Queen Victoria in 1851.
Open: Monday–Sunday 09.00–17.00 hrs.

HOHER MARKT

In Roman *Vindobona*, this was the site of the Forum (a short step from the city's appropriately named Marc-Aurel Strasse where Emperor Marcus Aurelius died in AD180). An air raid in 1945 exposed two Roman houses on Hoher Markt at No 3, and the excavations are now preserved for posterity in a tiny underground museum. A relief map, superimposed on today's street plan, shows how far the Roman garrison extended and offers an unusual insight into the vertical time-line of Vienna – strange to think that all these sunken layers were once the street level. Back at contemporary street level, the Nuptial Fountain in the middle of the square by Fischer von Erlach the Younger replaced an earlier version by his father.

◆
JOSEFSPLATZ
Hofburg, Augustinerstrasse
A beautiful baroque square bordered by the National Library and the adjoining Grosser and Kleiner Redoutensaal. At Josefsplatz 6 stands the Palais Pálffy (1675) and next to it, the Palais Pallavicini (1783). The statue in the centre of the square is of Maria Theresa's son, Emperor Joseph II. Built by Fischer von Erlach the Younger, to his father's plans, the National Library has a particularly handsome oval hall called the Prunksaal, decorated with frescos depicting the library's benefactors, in particular, Karl I. The hall houses more than 200,000 books, all of which are over 100 years old, plus 36,000 manuscripts and 8,000 early printed works as well as Prince Eugene of Savoy's library. On the library's third floor is a collection of antique globes. *Open*: Monday to Wednesday, Friday 11.00–12.00 hrs.

◆
JUDENPLATZ
Tucked behind the Böhmische Hofkanzlei (Bohemian Court

Alte Hofburg, home of emperors

AMOREM · MEVM · POPVLIS · MEIS

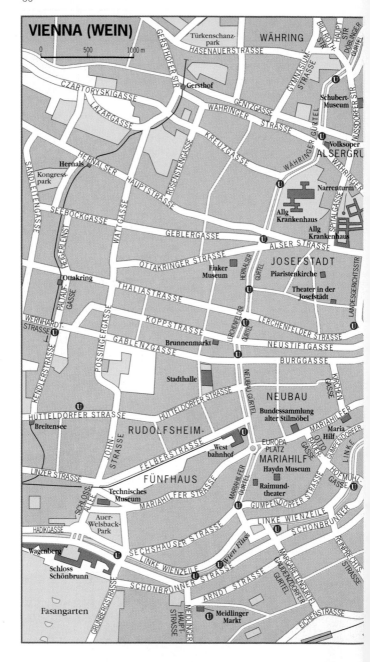

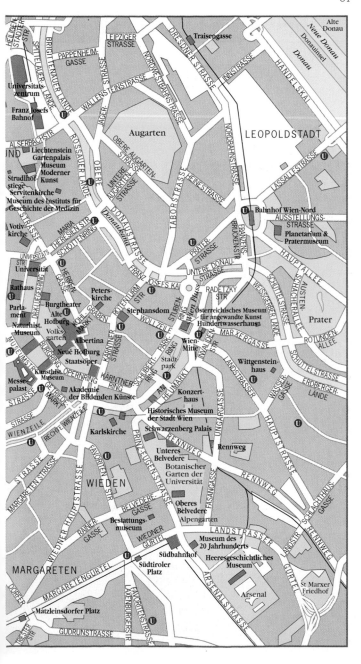

Chancery), Judenplatz was the heart of Vienna's Jewish ghetto during the Middle Ages. Its synagogue was torn down during a 1421 anti-semitic pogrom and the stones were carried away to build an extension of the Old University. The pogrom is commemorated in a 16th-century relief on the façade of Judenplatz 2, known as 'Jordanhof' after its original 15th-century owner, Jörg Jordan. There are several other fine

houses in the square; Mozart once lived here; and the celebrated architect, J B Fischer von Erlach died just off the square at Jordangasse 5 in 1723.

Reflection in the Kaiserappartements

◆◆◆
KAISERAPPARTEMENTS ✓

Hofburg, Michaelerplatz
The 45-minute tour of these grandiose Habsburg living quarters is a must. For sheer opulance, they are splendid, of course, full of gorgeous period furniture and decoration, tapestries and crystal chandeliers that literally do weigh in at around a ton. However, the most fascinating aspect of the tour is the chance to place historical figures in their true surroundings. Ranged around the In der Burg courtyard, there are three sets of inter-connecting state rooms open to the public running from the Reichskanzlei wing through to the Amalienburg. With 21 rooms in all, this was home to Franz Josef I and the Empress Elisabeth, plus a 'home from home' for Alexander I, Tsar of Russia, during the 1814–15 Congress of Vienna. Maria Theresa's apartments, across the courtyard in the Leopoldinischer wing, are the official residence of the Austrian President, and cannot be visited. Franz Josef's suite runs the length of the Reichskanzlei wing. His dining room is lined with Gobelin tapestries and leads into the Circle Room, where members of the Court gathered after dinner to discuss the day's affairs and to gossip. Smokers would withdraw to the Smoking Room next door. The Guardroom is followed by two audience chambers. The first was a waiting room; the second contains the lectern at which Franz Josef received petitioners. The Council Chamber is

WHAT TO SEE

The Habsburg Crown once united Spain and Austria

adorned with the famous Winterhalter portrait of Empress Elisabeth, aged 28, when she was widely recognised as one of the most beautiful women in Europe. Through a study, you reach the Emperor's bedroom with a simple iron bedstead and wooden bath tub – no damasked four-poster or revolutionary running water, just a modest coat of arms emblazoned on the water pitcher. Two salons bring

you to the corner of the building, and into Empress Elisabeth's living room/bedroom. Pretty and self-contained, with its own desk, prie-dieu and a bed (which was removed daily), there is also the Empress' private gymnasium, where she exercised every day to the mystification and downright disapproval of her court. There is a particularly gracious salon furnished in Louis XIV-style with Sèvres porcelain and fine landscape paintings, while an anteroom displays memorabilia surrounding the Empress' assassination by an Italian anarchist in Geneva in 1898. Alexander I's salon boasts some superior Gobelin tapestries from designs by Boucher, which were presented to Joseph II by his sister, Marie-Antoinette, and the study was later used by Karl I to draft his abdication document in 1918. Finally, the Banqueting Hall, with an impressive top table formally laid-up in Spanish style.

Open: Monday to Saturday 08.30–12.00 hrs and 12.30–16.00 hrs, Sunday 08.30–12.30 hrs.

◆◆◆
KAPUZINERKIRCHE ✓

Neuer Markt
Beneath the suitably austere surroundings of the Capuchin Church, founded by Empress Anna in 1618, lies one of the most extraordinary monuments to the Imperial Family, the Kaisergruft (Imperial Burial Vault). Since 1633, when the remains of Anna and her husband, Matthias I, were placed here, all but three of their successors have been laid to rest in one of the vault's 10 chambers. Of the three exceptions, Ferdinand II (1619–37) is buried at Graz; Frederick III (1637–57) has a sepulchre in St Stephen's; and Karl I 'The Last' (1916–18) is buried on Madeira where he lived in exile until his death in 1922. The interlinking chambers, visited in chronological order, provide a fascinating guide to styles through the ages, and to personal preferences such as

the strikingly modest copper coffin of Joseph II, ever-disdainful of pomp and frippery, compared with that of his parents – a double sarcophagus resplendent with angels, winged eagles, shrouded heads, cushions, crowns and garlands of flowers. From Anna and Matthias' Founders' Vault, you enter the Leopoldine Vault, where 12 of 16 sarcophagi were built for children, hence it is sometimes called the Angel Vault.

Highlight of the Caroline Vault is Karl VI's imposing tomb, designed by Balthasar Ferdinand Moll, supported by lions and decorated with coats of arms representing the Holy Roman Empire and its dominions. Moll was also responsible for Maria Theresa and Franz I's rococo-style resting place and several sarcophagi for the couple's offspring. The only non-royal buried in the vault is found here in a niche close to the family she

Imperial elegance: Kapuzinerkirche

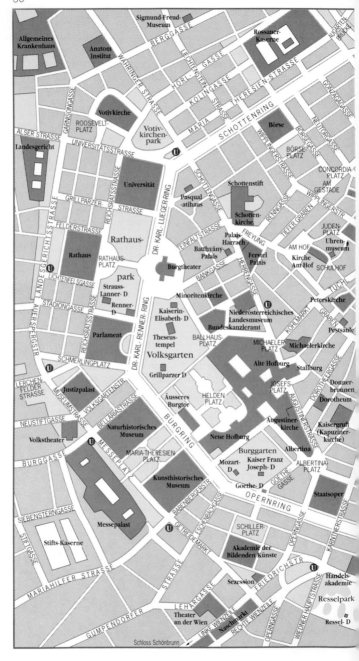

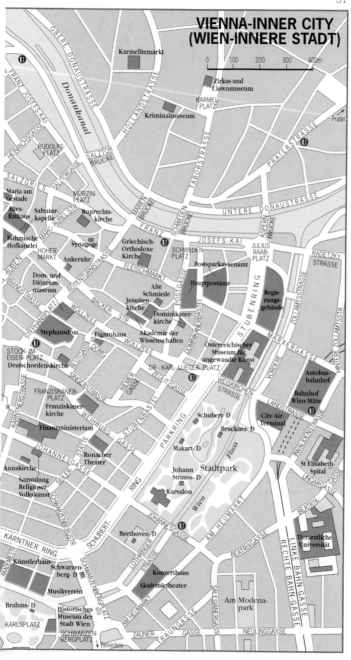

VIENNA-INNER CITY
(WIEN-INNERE STADT)

0   100   200   300   400m

Karmelitemarkt

Zirkus-und
Clownmuseum

KARMEL-
PLATZ

Kriminalmuseum

Prater

OBERE DONAUSTRASSE

Donaukanal

FRANZ JOSEFS-KAI

HEINRICHSGASSE

RUDOLFS-
PLATZ

SALZTOR-
BRUCKE

SALZGRIES

SALZTORGASSE

MORZIN-
PLATZ

HOLLANDSTRASSE

TABORSTRASSE

MAREN
BRUCKE

SCHWEDEN-
BRUCKE

PRATERSTRASSE

ASPERN
BRUCKE

UNTERE DONAUSTRASSE

Maria am
Gestade

Altes-
Rathaus

Salvator-
kapelle

Ruprechts-
kirche

MARC-AUREL-STR

FRANZ

JOSEFS-KAI

RADETZKY-
STRASSE

Böhmische
Hofkanzlei

HOHER
MARKT

Synagoge

Ankeruhr

Griechisch-
Orthodoxe
Kirche

SCHWEDEN-
PLATZ

JULIUS
RAAB-
PLATZ

AUBEN

BRANDSTRASSE

Dom- und
Diözesan-
museum

ROTENTURMSTRASSE

FLEISCHMARKT

Postsparkassenamt

ZOLLAMTSSTRASSE

STEPHANSPLATZ

Alte
Schmiede

POSTGASSE

Hauptpostamt

Regie-
rungs-
gebäude

Stephansdom

BACKER-
STR

Jesuiten-
kirche

Dominikaner-
kirche

Figarohaus

Akademie der
Wissenschaften

STUBENRING

MARXERGASSE

HINTERE ZOLLAMTSSTR

STOCK-IM-
EISEN-PLATZ

Deutschordenskirche

WOLLZEILE

DOMG

RIEMER-
GASSE

DR.-KARL-LUEGER-PLATZ

DOMINIKANERBASTEI

Österreichisches
Museum für
angewandte Kunst

VORDERE

Autobus-
bahnhof

FRANZISKANER-
PLATZ

SINGERSTRASSE

BLUTGASSE

ZEDLITZGASSE

WEISKIRCHEN-
STRASSE

Bahnhof
Wien-Mitte

KARNTNERSTRASSE

Franziskaner-
kirche

Finanzministerium

STUBEN-
GASSE

WEIHBURG-

Schubert- D

Bruckner- D

City-Air-
Terminal

LANDSTRASSE

INVALIDENSTRASSE

JOHANNES

STALTE

Ronacher
Theater

Makart- D

St Elisabeth-
Spital

UNGARGASSE

Annakirche

SEILER

Johann
Strauss- D

Stadtpark

BEATRIX

GASSE

Sammlung
Religiöser
Volkskunst

SCHWARZENBERGSTR

RING

Kursalon

Wien

Fluss

PARKRING

KARNTNER RING

SCHUBERT-

JOHANNESGASSE

Beethoven- D

AM HEUMARKT

BEATRIXGASSE

RECHTE BAHN GASSE

LINKE BAHN GASSE

Tierärztliche
Universität

Künstlerhaus

AKADEMIESTR

Schwarzen-
berg- D

SCHWARZENBERGPLATZ

LOTHRINGER
STRASSE

Konzerthaus

Akademietheater

SALESIANERGASSE

Am Modena-
park

Musikverein

Brahms- D

Historisches
Museum der
Stadt Wien

KARLSPLATZ

SCHWARZEN-
BERGPLATZ

ZAUNER-
GASSE

TRAUNGASSE

AM HEUMARKT

NEULINGGASSE

Belvedere

served so dutifully. Karoline Füchs, who died in 1754, was the Empress' governess and was largely responsible for her upbringing. She remained with the family all her life. Franz II was the last Holy Roman Emperor and has his own vault. He renounced the Holy Roman crown in 1806, and became plain old Emperor Franz I of Austria. Ferdinand I's vault, the Tuscan Vault and the New Vault house numerous Habsburg relatives, while Franz Josef is placed between his wife and tragic son, Crown Prince Rudolf,

Echoes of Rome at the Karlskirche

who both predeceased him. *Open*: daily 09.30–16.00 hrs.

◆◆◆
KARLSKIRCHE
Karlsplatz
Just outside the Ringstrasse, but still within Vienna's First District, the Karlskirche is the city's finest baroque church. It was commissioned by Karl VI to mark the end of the plague epidemic in 1713, and is dedicated to St Charles Borromeo, noted for his work among plague victims in Italy. The overall design was master-minded by J B Fischer von Erlach, and the foundations were laid in 1716 – foundations

strong enough to withstand a handful of very close calls from air raids during World War II. The Karls-kirche proved to be von Erlach the Elder's swansong, and it was completed by his son, J E Fischer von Erlach in 1739, funded by contributions extracted from each of the countries aligned to the Holy Roman Empire. The broad façade, flanked by twin campaniles, is notable for its massive triumphal pillars inspired by Trajan's Column in Rome, and one of the architect's favourite devices. They are adorned with spiral ribbons of decoration depicting scenes from St Charles Borromeo's life, and support replicas of the Imperial crown. At the centre, a Greek portico is topped with a relief illustrating victory over the plague. Rising sheer above the vast oval body of the church, its great copper dome reaches a height of 235 feet (72m). Pierced by several windows, the interior frescos by Johann Michael Rottmayr are particularly well displayed above the staggeringly ornate high altar showing St Charles ascending into a veritable tempest of golden clouds and heavenly rays. The frescos are similarly concerned with St Charles, but note also the censorial angel setting light to a copy of Luther's Bible. Do not miss Gaetano Fanti's splendid *trompe l'oeil* paintings, Daniel Gran's *St Elisabeth* by the high altar, and Rottmayr's *St Cecilia* decorating the organ case with a host of angelic music makers.

Neon lights in Kärntnerstrasse

WHAT TO SEE

◆◆
KÄRNTNERSTRASSE

You really cannot miss a stroll along the Inner City's most fashionable shopping street. It was always the main north-south thoroughfare, a central artery linking the twin poles of the city, with the Stephansdom at one end and the Staatsoper at the other. Prince Metternich once said 'The Balkans begin at the Kärntnerstrasse', in the days when Vienna literally was a frontier city. Now a pedestrianised precinct, you will find a host of pavement cafés here.

◆◆◆
KUNSTHISTORISCHES MUSEUM

Maria-Theresien-Platz
Top of your list of museums, the Museum of Fine Arts is on a par with the Louvre and the Prado. Its collections are absolutely magnificent, thanks to the acquisitive Habsburgs. A single visit will not do this national gallery justice, so if you cannot afford the time to return, pick an era and style of art that most appeals to you and concentrate your energies. Antiquities, the Egyptian and Oriental sections, and the main sculpture collections are on the ground floor; on the first floor, paintings from the Dutch and Flemish schools are flanked to one side by German and English artists, with the Italians, Spanish and French on the other. Among the classical antiquities, you will find Greek, Cypriot, Etruscan, Roman and early Christian art, plus items from the period of the Germanic Migrations. Of

especial interest on the decorative arts front are the Ionic, Attic and Italian vases; the beautiful *Gemma Augustea* onyx cameo which is thought to date from the 1st century AD, showing the Emperor Augustus welcoming home his son Tiberius after defeating the Pannonia (ie: Austrian) barbarians; the 12th-century Wilten Chalice; and Benvenuto Cellini's fabulous gold-enamelled salt cellar, which was designed for King Francis I of France. On the first floor, fans of the Flemish School are in luck. Almost half of Pieter Brueghel the Elder's surviving work is on display here – an amazing collection which includes many of his peasant themes such as *Peasant Games* and *Peasant Wedding* along with the more religious themes *Christ Carrying the Cross* and *Building the Tower of Babel*. Do not miss Hans Holbein's celebrated portrait of Jane Seymour, one of Henry VIII's wives who did not lose her head, and Anthony Van Dyck's dramatic rendition entitled *Young Field Commander*. Jan Vermeer's *Allegory of Painting* shows the artist painting a shy young woman; there is a Rembrandt *Self Portrait*; and Peter Paul Rubens is well represented by more than 30 canvasses, including a self portrait, that of his second wife, and many more. Albrecht Dürer is represented by a dignified portrait of *Emperor Maximilian*, a sophisticated work as intensely spiritual as his *The Holy Trinity Surrounded by All Saints*. Among the Italian masters on display, Titian's madonnas are exquisite

The Kunsthistorisches Museum

and Tintoretto's *Suzanna in her Bath* is one of his finest pictures. Giorgione's *Three Philosophers* is one of the rare surviving examples of his work; there are several charming scenes from the 16th-century Venetian painter, Veronese; and Raphael's *Madonna and Greenery*. The Velázquez collection, which almost matches that in Madrid, includes the *Infanta Margarita Teresa* and *King Philip IV and Queen Isabella*. For superb views of Vienna, look to the Bellotto (Canaletto's nephew) views of the Freyung, Neuer Markt and

WHAT TO SEE

*Keep a straight face in
Michaelerplatz*

City Seen from the Belvedere.
British painter Thomas
Gainsborough has a *Suffolk
Landscape* hanging here.
*Napoleon Crossing the St
Bernard Pass* is one of the few
Davids to be seen outside the
Louvre. In its entirety, this
museum achieves what few
other art museums can – a
balanced and integrated
presentation of European art that
will have you raring to see
more.
Open: daily except Monday
10.00–18.00 hrs, Thursday to
21.00 hrs.

LOBMEYR
Kärntnerstrasse 26
Founded in 1823, Lobmeyr's
have reigned supreme as the
city's premier glassmakers.
Official suppliers of chandeliers
to the Austrian Court, they
produced the first electrically lit
chandelier in 1883, and their
sparkling successes illuminate
such diverse establishments as
the Kremlin and New York's
Metropolitan Opera House.
Above the shop, you will find a
superb glass museum.
Open: Monday to Friday
09.00–18.00 hrs, Saturday
09.00–13.00 hrs.

LOOS-HAUS
Michaelerplatz 5
Architect Adolph Loos' austere
1910 department store design,
with its clean lines and functional
appearance, raised storms of
public protest as it grew across
the street from the Michaeler

wing of the Hofburg. Franz Josef
hated it so much that he refused
to leave the Hofburg by the
Michaelertor exit, and
complained vociferously about
the 'windows without eyebrows'
(they don't have lintels).

MARIA AM GESTADE
Salvatorgasse
A lovely 14th-century Gothic
church built on Roman
foundations. The west façade is
particularly impressive and
there is outstanding 14th-
century stained glass in the
choir.

MICHAELERKIRCHE
Michaelerplatz
Once the court parish church,
parts of which date from the
13th century. Look out for
Matielli's statue of *St Michael*
over the portal, and the unusual
Gothic choir.

The Naturhistorisches Museum

◆
MUSEUM FÜR ANGEWANDTE KUNST
Stubenring 5
The Museum of Applied Art displays a broad-ranging selection of examples from numerous genres including enamel and goldsmith's work, glass painting, lace, furniture and carpets. Recommended viewing for anyone with an interest in decorative arts.
Open: daily except Monday 10.00–18.00 hrs, Thursday to 21.00 hrs.

◆◆
NATURHISTORISCHES MUSEUM
Maria-Theresien-Platz
Fine Natural History Museum with interesting displays covering mineralogy, botany, zoology, anthropology and pre-history, as well as an outstanding collection of precious stones. In the pre-history section, you will see the 20,000 year-old *Venus of Willendorf* statuette, and finds from burial sites near Hallstatt. There is also a special children's corner.
Open: Wednesday to Monday 09.00–18.00 hrs.

◆◆
NEUE HOFBURG
Heldenplatz
Part of Franz Josef's plans for an extension to the Hofburg, today the Neue Hofburg houses a congress centre, the National Library reading rooms and several museums. The **Museum für Völkerkunde** (Ethnological Museum) is certainly worth a visit. Among the ethnological objects on display from non-European civilisations you will see Montezuma's head plumes,

WHAT TO SEE

shield and standard, and Benin bronzes.

Other collections housed in the Neue Hofburg range from armour and musical instruments to the Ephesus Museum, with its treasures from the famous Greek-Turkish excavation site, and the Museum of Austrian Culture.

Open: daily except Tuesday 10.00–16.00 hrs.

◆
PETERSKIRCHE
(*off Graben*)

A superb example of graceful baroque design, this church, with its oval nave and impressive carvings, is the work of Gabriele Montani and Johann Lukas von Hildebrandt.

PLATZ AM HOF

The Old City's largest square has done service in its time as a market place, execution site, jousting stadium, and is the spot where the 12th-century Babenberg dukes built their fortress (where No 7 now stands). The Mariensäule (Mary's Column) was erected in 1667 to celebrate Austria's victory over the Swedes in the Thirty Years War. In the Gothic-cum-baroque Am Hof Church, Emperor Franz II threw off the cloak of the Holy Roman Empire in 1806, and became Emperor Franz I of the Austrian Empire. Theodor Latour,

Platz Am Hof: peace and quiet in the centre of the old city

then Minister of War, was hanged from a lamp post in the middle of the square by Viennese revolutionaries in 1848. A plaque in the square's southwest corner honours Swiss philanthropist, Henry Dunant who was so disturbed by the bloodiness of the Battle of Solferino in 1859 that he founded the Red Cross.

◆
RATHAUS
Rathausplatz
The attractive town hall, completed in 1872, bears more than a passing resemblance to its sister in Brussels. Both were designed by fashionable 19th-century architect Friedrich Schmidt, whose concern with style sometimes overrode more

practical considerations such as the windows, which are so small that unfortunate civil servants had to work all day by candlelight. The figure atop the town hall, the Rathaus Man, has become something of a Viennese symbol. Providing there are no sessions in progress, guided tours are given Monday to Friday at 13.00 hrs.

> **New Year's Eve**
> On New Year's Eve *the* place to be for a street party is outside the **Rathaus**. From 10.00 in the morning to 02.00 hrs the next day, entertainment includes fire eaters, performers on stilts and dancing demonstrations in the marquee.

◆◆◆
SAMMLUNG ALTER MUSIKINSTRUMENTE ✓

Neue Hofburg, Heldenplatz
Composed of several collections, notably those of the musical 16th-century Archduke Ferdinand of Tyrol and Vienna's Gesellschaft der Musikfreunde (Music Lovers' Society), the Collection of Old Musical Instruments is a priceless record of the development of western music and some of its greatest exponents.
The earliest examples on display, which date from the 15th century, include Italian violas and Archduke Ferdinand's own finely wrought trumpet, made for him by Antoni Schnitzer of Nuremburg in 1581. Woodwind instruments range from a 1501 bass flute and simple recorders to a 16th-century local curiosity from the Tyrol called a 'Tartolten'

WHAT TO SEE

with a set of five oboe-like pipes. Among the plucked instruments, you will find harps, lutes and zithers; while stringed instruments run the gamut from the sublime (if not entirely practical) to the workaday by way of an unusual violin which is made of tortoiseshell and a hurdy-gurdy.

The keyboard collection is perhaps the highlight here, not only for its spectacular range and famous name makers, but also for the historic associations with great composers. Among clavichords, cembalos, uprights and spinets, there is a grand piano by Erard Frères presented to Beethoven in 1803; another, by Graf, was presented to Schumann on the occasion of his wedding in 1839, and later donated by Brahms. You can see Mahler's Bluthner; a square table piano commandeered by Schubert when staying with friends; Haydn's harpsichord; and Liszt's harmonium. The museum sometimes lends out instruments to add authenticity to period concerts, some of which are staged in the grand Marble Hall.

Open: daily except Tuesday 10.00–18.00 hrs.

◆◆◆
SCHATZKAMMER ✓

Hofburg, Schweizerhof
Buried in the heart of the Hofburg, in a tower once patrolled by Swiss Guards, the Habsburgs' Treasury is one of the richest in Europe. Ever since the 16th century, the Habsburg emperors have stored their treasures in the Hofburg, building a collection of inestimable value and tremendous historic and artistic significance. Housed in a suite of rooms, the collection is divided between secular exhibits which are arranged in groups of related type, and sacred objects which are displayed in chronological order. The secular section traces a fascinating path through the ceremonial lives of the Habsburg emperors. There is Maximilian I's investiture sword, which was used at fealty ceremonies, when subjects were bound into the feudal system by swearing their loyalty and that of their descendants to the ruling house; a display of embroidered baptismal robes including gold christening vessels; the coats of arms and insignia of the Order of the Golden Fleece; and heirlooms, such as a legendary unicorn's horn (a narwhal in this case) presented to Ferdinand I by King Sigismund of Poland. However, the most spectaular pieces on show are the crowns and court regalia, where the octagonal Imperial Crown reserves pride of place. This 10th-century masterpiece was probably made in Germany for the coronation of Otto the Great, and passed into the hands of the Habsburg family in the 13th century. Studded with pearls and precious stones, the crown is decorated with delicate enamelled panels and traversed from back to front by a single scallop-edged arc with a bejewelled cross raised above the central browpiece: certainly fit for an emperor.

Among the sacred treasures on display, you will find medieval relics, fine gold and silver work, magnificent vestments including those given to Joseph II by Pope Pius VI, carvings, statues and liturgical vessels in a range of different styles from the Renaissance through baroque to rococo.

Open: daily except Tuesday 10.00–18.00 hrs, Thursday to 21.00 hrs.

◆
SCHWEIZERHOF
Hofburg
Named for the Swiss Guard once housed here, this part of the Hofburg dates from the 13th century, when it was built by Bohemian King Ottokar to defend himself (unsuccessfully) against Rudolf von Habsburg. By

An ornate façade: the Sezession Building was home of the Jugendstil

WHAT TO SEE

the archway, you will see the pulleys through which the drawbridge chains were lowered.

◆
SEZESSION
Friedrichstrasse 12
Known as the 'Temple of the Jugendstil' (the Viennese Art Nouveau movement), this extraordinary building was designed by Josef Olbrich and built in six months during 1898. During the 1890's, a group of young artists, led by Gustav Klimt, broke away from the traditional Künstlerhaus school of artists and founded the Artists' Union, Sezession. This was their exhibition gallery, and it also hosted shows by sympathetic foreign artists such as Beardsley (1899), and Glasgow designer Charles Rennie Mackintosh (1900). Topped by an eye-catching sphere, the façade bears the inscription *Der Zeit ihre Kunst, der Kunst ihre Freiheit* (To every age its art, to art its freedom). The restored basement contains Klimt's notable *Beethoven Frieze.*
Open: Tuesday to Friday 10.00–18.00 hrs, weekend 10.00–16.00 hrs.

Spanische Reitschule

◆◆◆
SPANISCHE REITSCHULE ✓

Hofburg (entrance on Josefsplatz)
A Viennese institution spanning
some 400 years, the Spanish
Riding School's performing
stallions remain one of the most
beloved images of the city. The
famous Lipizzaner horses,
named for the stud in Lipizza
(Yugoslavia) where they were
bred until 1918, were first
introduced by Maximilian II in
the 16th century. Originally a
Spanish strain, they were
crossed with Italian and Berber
horses before an Arab strain
was introduced in the 18th
century. During World War II,
the Riding School and its horses
were evacuated from Vienna,
and almost disappeared for
ever in battle-torn
Czechoslovakia. The stud was
saved in the nick of time by a
horse-loving US general,
George Patton, after a plea from
the School's director, Colonel
Alois Podhajsky, and today's
Lipizzaners are raised in the
Styrian town of Piber.
Lipizzaner foals are born a
mousey grey-brown colour, and
do not gain their pure white
adult coat until they are at least
four years old. At four, the
stallions are moved from the
stud to stables in Vienna, and
begin a four-year training
programme. Starting with
ground exercises (trots, steps,
pirouettes), they gradually build
up to off-ground exercises
which require an extraordinary
degree of balance and skill.
Performances take place in the
magnificent baroque
Winterreitschule (Winter
Riding School), where the riders
still perform in the traditional
uniform of dark brown tailcoat,
buckskin breeches, high boots
and bicorn hats. Karl VI staged
the first riding displays here,
and encouraged the finest
horsemen of the Court to
compete against each other for
amusement, while the intricacies
of *haute école* were taught to
young nobles alongside more
warlike cavalry exercises. Karl
VI still presides over the
Lipizzaners' equestrian ballet
today – the riders dutifully salute
his portrait above the Emperor's
Box at the start and finish of each
show.
Performances: from March to
June, November to December,
and occasionally during
September and October, on
Sunday at 10.45 hrs; plus April
to June most Wednesdays at
19.00 hrs. Written orders for
tickets (pay on collection) well in
advance to: **Spanische
Reitschule**, Hofburg, A-1010
Vienna. No reservations for
Morning Exercise, February to
June, September and November
to December Tuesday to
Saturday 10.00–12.00 hrs.
Tickets are sold at the entrance
in the inner courtyard of the
Imperial Palace.

◆◆
STAATSOPER
Opernring 2
The Opera House opened in
1869, with a performance of
Mozart's *Don Giovanni*, and
provided a glittering showcase
for the musical extravaganzas
which marked the final decades
of Imperial Vienna. Almost
completely destroyed by World

Stephandom's tiled roof

War II bombs, the Opera House was rebuilt in the 1950s (once Austria had regained her independence), and the new edifice retains the ornate classicism of the original. There are guided tours daily in July and August at 10.00, 11.00, 13.00, 14.00 and 15.00 hrs and on request between September and June.

◆
STALLBURG
Reitschulgasse 2
Vienna's finest Renaissance building, the Stallburg was commissioned by Ferdinand I in 1558, and intended as a palace for his son, Archduke Maximilian. It was Maximilian, who, as Emperor Maximilian II, introduced the Spanish Riding

School's famous 'Silver Stallions', and thus it seems entirely appropriate that part of the Stallburg is now the Lipizzaner Mews, where the famous horses of the Spanish Riding School are stabled. It is linked to the Winterreitschule by a passage. The stables, however, are not open to visitors (also see **Spanische Reitschule** and **Winterreitschule**, page 49).

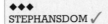
STEPHANSDOM ✓

Stephansplatz
The dominant landmark of the Inner City, St Stephen's Cathedral was founded during

the reign of the Bohemian King Ottokar in the 13th century, on the site of several earlier Christian churches. The building represents eight centuries of continuous construction, starting with the Romanesque west façade, which features the massive Riesentor (Giant's Gate). This is the main entrance, flanked by the Heidentürme (Pagan Towers). After the initial surprise of discovering the 'Dom' has, in fact, a steep-sided roof covered with coloured tiles, the most striking aspect of the exterior is the magnificent South Tower, part of the cathedral's 14th-century Gothic transformation. Known locally as the 'Steffl', the South Tower's dramatic steeple soars to a height of 450 feet (137m). It was

originally planned as one of a pair, but funds were never forthcoming to complete its northern sister, the Eagle Tower, which became the bell tower, and is strikingly crowned with a copper cupola.

The cathedral interior is equally imposing, stretching 300 feet (92m) from end to end beneath a towering vaulted roof supported on nine pairs of pillars decorated with interesting life-size figures. To the left of Giant's Gate the Tirna Chapel is the burial place of soldier-prince, Eugene of Savoy, for whom the Belvedere was built. In the centre of the nave, Anton Pilgram's 1515 sandstone pulpit

Still dominating the city skyline – the Stephansdom's Gothic glory

WHAT TO SEE

depicts the four Fathers of the Church, and the artist himself peeping through a window under the stairs. (He also features below the organ loft.) Off the north aisle, there is a lift to the Pummerin Bell in the Eagle Tower – just the place for a spectacular bird's-eye view of the city.

Then you can descend to the Catacombs, lined with copper urns containing the intestines of the Habsburg emperors. In the north apse of the choir, you will find the carved wooden Wiener Neustadter altar (1447); in the south apse, Friedrich III's red marble sepulchre. Honoured for making the city a bishopric in 1469, the initials of the emperor's optimistic slogan, AEIOU (roughly translated it means 'Austria is destined to rule the world'), appear on the choir stalls.

Guided tours of the Cathedral are given Monday to Saturday at 10.30 and 15.00 hrs, Sunday at 15.00 hrs.

Evening guided tours are available July to September, Saturday 19.00 hrs.

The catacombs are open daily and may be visited on a guided tour at 10.00, 11.00, 11.30 hrs and 14.00, 14.30, 15.30, 16.00, 16.30 hrs. The North Tower (visitors gain access by lift) daily 09.00–18.00 hrs, 17.30 hrs in winter.

The South Tower is open daily 09.00–17.30 hrs.

◆
STOCK IM EISEN PLATZ
extension of Stephansplatz
The gnarled tree trunk preserved in the small square

(at the corner of Graben) is the last remaining vestige of the Wienerwald from the days when the Vienna Woods actually bordered this part of town. In the Middle Ages, travelling journeymen would drive a nail into it for good luck – many of these nails have survived.

◆
UHRENMUSEUM
Schulhof 2
A must for horologists, the Clock Museum displays a world-class collection of antique and modern timepieces from around the globe. Travelling clocks,

Votivkirche seen beyond the Rathaus

cuckoo clocks, carriage clocks, pendants and watches plus Rutschmann's magnificent 1769 astronomical clock.
Open: Tuesday to Sunday 09.00–16.30 hrs.

◆
VOTIVKIRCHE
Rooseveltplatz
Built in the 19th century to designs by Heinrich von Ferstel, this French cathedral-style church is dedicated to the Divine Saviour in recognition of Franz Josef's survival of the 1853 assassination attempt. There are several military monuments dating from the days when this was a garrison church, and the baptismal chapel contains the Renaissance tomb of Count Niklas Salm, one of Vienna's defenders during the Turkish siege of 1529.

Outer City Attractions

◆
ALTE DONAU
cross the Reichsbrücke and follow Wagramerstrasse
If the sun is out this closed off arm of the river, known as the 'Old Danube', could (at a pinch) be described as 'blue'. It's the city's own little recreation centre offering sailing, fishing and swimming. Subway U1.

◆◆
BEETHOVEN MEMORIAL ROOMS
Probusgasse 6 and Doblinger Hauptstrasse 92
Beethoven had numerous homes in Vienna during his 35 year residency, and these two are found in the 19th District. Already suffering partial deafness, the

VIENNA-ENVIRONS

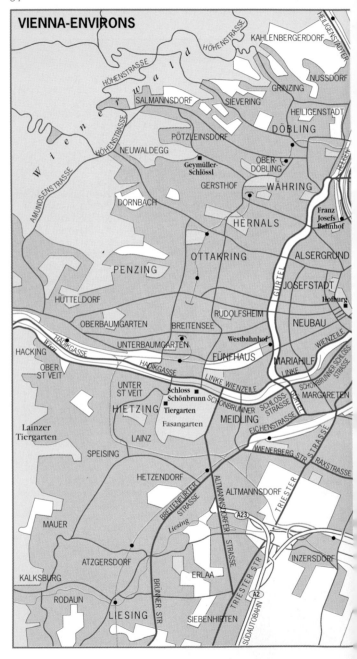

KAHLENBERGERDORF

HÖHENSTRASSE

HÖHENSTRASSE

NUSSDORF

GRINZING

SALMANNSDORF

SIEVERING

HEILIGENSTADT

W i e n e r w a l d

PÖTZLEINSDORF

DÖBLING

HÖHENSTRASSE

NEUWALDEGG

OBER-
DOBLING

Geymüller-
Schlössl

WÄHRING

GERSTHOF

AMUNDSENSTRASSE

DORNBACH

Franz
Josefs
Bahnhof

HERNALS

OTTAKRING

ALSERGRUND

PENZING

JOSEFSTADT

GURTEL

HÜTTELDORF

Hofburg

RUDOLFSHEIM

NEUBAU

OBERBAUMGARTEN

BREITENSEE

Westbahnhof

WIENZEILE

Wien

HADIKGASSE

UNTERBAUMGARTEN

MARIAHILF

HACKING

HADIKGASSE

FÜNFHAUS

LINKE

SCHÖNBRUNNER SCHLOSS
STRASSE

OBER
ST VEIT

LINKE WIENZEILE

SCHÖNBRUNNER STRASSE

UNTER
ST VEIT

Schloss
Schönbrunn

SCHONBRUNNER

MARGARETEN

SCHLOSS
STRASSE

GURTEL

HIETZING

Tiergarten

MEIDLING

Lainzer
Tiergarten

Fasangarten

EICHENSTRASSE

LAINZ

WIENERBERG STR

SPEISING

RAXSTRASSE

STRASSE

HETZENDORF

ALTMANNSDORF

TRIESTER

BREITENFURTER
STRASSE

ALTMANNSDORFER

A23

MAUER

Liesing

INZERSDORF

STRASSE

ATZGERSDORF

ERLAA

TRIESTER STR

KALKSBURG

BRUNNER STR

A2

RODAUN

LIESING

SIEBENHIRTEN

SÜDAUTOBAHN

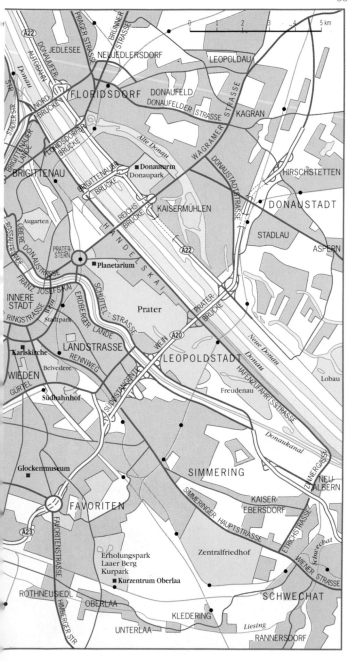

composer moved to Heiligenstadt in 1800, hoping that the park's waters might provide a miraculous cure. While at the Probusgasse house he wrote the *Heiligenstadter Testament*, a bitter diatribe against his deafness, yet less than a year later he completed the marvellous Second Symphony. *Open*: Tuesday to Sunday 09.00–12.15 hrs and 13.00–16.30 hrs.

◆◆◆

BELVEDERE ✓

Prinz-Eugen-Strasse 27
Prince Eugene of Savoy's

magnificent palace overlooks the Inner City from the Third District, planted amid Dominique Girard's spectacular terraced gardens, embellished by waterfalls, fountains and statues of mythical figures. The prince was of mixed continental ancestry and grew up at the French court of Louis XIV. Destined for a career in the clergy, the young Eugene ran away to join the Austrian army as an ordinary soldier. He fought his first battle in 1683, and rose to become Commander-in-Chief, with the rank of Field Marshal by the

Turkish War of 1697. Success brought wealth, which the Prince used to fund his passion for art and literature – his collections now grace the shelves and walls of the National Library and the Albertina. Johann Lukas von Hildebrandt built the Unteres (Lower) Belvedere as a summer home for the Prince in 1714. Today, it houses the **Österreichisches Barockmuseum** (Baroque Museum) which celebrates the 18th-century flowering of Austrian art in considerable

Sphinx in the Belvedere's garden

style. Highlights include the Rottmayr Room; the lofty Marble Hall with lashings of stucco and a ceiling fresco by Altomonte; and the dazzling Hall of Mirrors where Balthasar Permoser's sculpture *Apotheosis of Prince Eugene* depicts the Field Marshal as Hercules, spurning Envy and modestly attempting to silence Fame's trumpet. The second museum on the lower level is the **Museum Mittelalterlicher Österreichischer Kunst** (Austrian Medieval Art) which is displayed in the Orangerie. The collection has been gathered

WHAT TO SEE

Hildebrandt's Upper Belvedere

from around the country, and features masterpieces of wood and stone carving, paintings and altar pieces.

The Oberes (Upper) Belvedere, completed in 1723, was the prince's banquet hall. (It was also where Austria's post-war independence treaty was signed in 1955.) Now the gracious reception rooms play host to the **Österreichische Galerie der 19 und 20. Jahrhunderts** (Austrian Modern Art), where the rise of Jugendstil is clearly reflected against the background of early 19th-century classicism.

Perhaps the most expressive works are found on the second floor with Gustav Klimt's *The Kiss* and *Frau Bloch*; also Egon Schiele's *The Family* and *The Artist's Wife*.

Visitors to the Kunsthistorisches Museum may have seen there Bellotto's painting *City seen from the Belvedere*. Stand now on the terrace of the Upper Belvedere and you will see that little has changed. A stroll

around the top side of the Upper Belvedere, past a huge pond, will bring you to the alpine garden; and on the Prinz-Eugen-Strasse side of the Belvedere is the custodian's annexe where Bruckner was allowed to live the last few months of his life.

Open: Tuesday to Sunday 10.00–17.00 hrs.

In summer, check for details of the evening *son et lumière* displays.

◆

DONAUPARK

across Reichsbrücke, off Hubertusdammstrasse

Between the Old and New Danube, this green open space offers gardens and a lake, plus several areas set aside for sporting activities. If you take a ride on the chair lift, there is a terrific view of the whole park. Or enjoy a meal with a view atop the 827 foot (252m) Donauturm, where two revolving restaurants give you a splendid 360° panorama of the city and surroundings: an interesting way to eat out.

FREUD'S HOUSE
Berggasse 19
A chance for students of Sigmund
Freud to take a voyeuristic trip
around the master's consulting
rooms faithfully reconstructed in
this Ninth District house where
he lived from 1891 until the
arrival of the Nazis in 1938. The
museum contains his original
furniture and possessions
including hats and initialled
suitcases, all placed in their
original positions, as well as
photographs, documents and
letters to Jung.
Open: daily 09.00–16.00 hrs.

GEYMÜLLER-SCHLÖSSL
Khevenhüllerstrasse 2
Built for a well-to-do banker, this
19th-century villa has been
restored and now houses the
Sobek Clock and Watch
Collection. There are some 200
clocks on display, illustrating
fashions from the baroque period
through to the mid-19th century.
Open: March–November
Tuesday, Wednesday, Friday–
Sunday 10.00–17.00 hrs. Guided
tour Sunday at 15.00 hrs.

HAYDN MUSEUM
Haydngasse 19
Haydn's home for the last 12
years of his life until his death in
1809, and where he composed
the oratorios *The Creation* and
The Seasons. The museum
displays documents, manuscripts
and memorabilia associated
with the composer, including a
death mask. There is also a
Brahms Memorial Room.
Open: Tuesday to Sunday 09.00–
12.15 hrs and 13.00–14.30 hrs.

HISTORISCHES MUSEUM DER STADT WIEN
Karlsplatz 4
Everything you could wish to
know about Viennese history is
displayed here, in the Fourth
District. On each floor of the
museum there is a model of the
city in its various stages of
development, together with
artefacts from the relevant
period, from Roman clay pots to
street lights, stained glass
rescued from St Stephen's, to
20th-century art. There are set
pieces which create a
microcosm of contemporary life,
complete with furnishings, art,
costume and even the games
people played.
Open: Tuesday to Sunday
09.00–13.00 hrs.

JOSEPHINUM
Währingerstrasse 25
Not for the faint-hearted, the
Josephinum was founded by
Joseph II in 1785 as a teaching
faculty for army doctors. It now
contains the Museum of the
History of Medicine, well-
furnished with gruesome
exhibits illustrating the progress
of medical science over the
ages.
Open: Monday to Friday
09.00–15.00 hrs.

MUSEUM DES 20 JAHRHUNDERTS
Schweizergarten, beyond the Belvedere
Housed in a steel and glass
pavilion designed by Karl
Schwanzer for the 1958 Brussels
World Fair, the 20th Century
Museum displays the work of

WHAT TO SEE

contemporary artists and recent masters, from Klee and Munch to Kandinsky and Wotruba. The gardens contain a strong sculpture collection with exhibits by Rodin, Henry Moore, Giacometti and Calder's distinctive brightly coloured mobiles. The Tourist Office can

Riesenrad: a really big wheel

provide details of current visiting exhibitions.
Open: Thursday to Tuesday 10.00–18.00 hrs.

♦♦♦
PRATER ✓

Praterstrasse
Where the Viennese go to let their hair down, the Prater is the city's amusement park. There are over 3,000 acres (1,214 hectares), once fenced in by Maximilian II as a hunting reserve, and first opened to the public in 1766.
Silhouetted against the sky is the Prater's most famous landmark, the giant **Riesenrad** (Ferris Wheel) erected for the 1896 World Fair. Destroyed in World War II and rebuilt in 1946, to measure 200 feet (60m) in diameter and weigh around 425 tons, it affords a magical view of the city, and starred alongside Orson Welles' Harry Lime in the 1949 film *The Third Man*. There is plenty going on at ground level too, with roundabouts, rollercoasters, dodgems, skittles and a miniature railway. You can watch swordswallowers and stilt-walkers going through their paces, or visit the suggestively named **Lusthaus** (Pleasure Pavilion) café-restaurant in a former hunting lodge rebuilt by Joseph II in 1782.
Close to the Wheel on Hauptallee, the **Planetarium** is worth a visit – it sometimes provides shows, so check if any are scheduled. It also houses the Prater Museum (*open:* Tuesday to Friday 09.00–12.15 hrs and 13.00–16.30 hrs. Saturday and Sunday 14.00–18.30 hrs).

Schönbrunn from the Gloriette

◆◆◆
SCHÖNBRUNN ✓

Schönbrunner Schlossstrasse 13
In 1696, Leopold I commissioned
J B Fischer von Erlach to build a
magnificent Imperial palace on
the Gloriette Hill, facing the site
of the present palace. The site
was changed and the plans
scaled down to a summer palace,
which was completed in 1730,
and used as a hunting lodge by
Karl VI. It is with his daughter,
Maria Theresa, that the palace is
most closely associated, for she
far preferred the gentler

WHAT TO SEE

atmosphere of Schönbrunn to that of the gloomy Hofburg. Architect Nikolaus Pacassi was given the task of converting the masculine lodge into a palace fit for the empress and found an attractive balance both suitably sumptuous, but intimate, too. A guided tour of the palace interior reveals several surprisingly homely touches, such as the empress' breakfast room, decorated with her own needlework, and the Porcelain Room where several of the Indian ink drawings are by members of the Imperial family. Mozart, aged six, gave his first royal recital in the glittering Hall of Mirrors, where Maria Theresa also swore

Schönbrunn, Habsburg hideaway

in her ministers. The round Chinese Room decorated with lacquered oriental panels, was used for 'secret' dinners. To avoid untimely interruptions by servants, a fully laid table would simply rise from the middle of the floor. Maria Theresa's bedroom decorated with Brussels tapestries was renamed the Napoleon Room when the French emperor stayed at Schönbrunn on his way to the Battle of Austerlitz. Later, his only legitimate son, the Duke of Reichstadt, died here of tuberculosis aged only 21. His death mask and stuffed pet bird

are on display. There are opulent ballrooms, a room of Persian miniatures, the state dining room, and Franz Josef's modest quarters. He also preferred Schönbrunn to the Hofburg, and was born and died here. The magnificent 500 acre park and gardens were laid out in French baroque style by Jean Trebet in 1705. Later additions included the graceful Gloriette colonnade designed by Von Hohenberg in 1775. From this high point of the park, the panorama extends north to Vienna, and south across the Wienerwald. The park is ornamented with fountains, statues of mythological figures and hidden arbours. Follies include the 'Roman Ruins', custom-built in 1778. Not far away is the Schöner Brunnen (beautiful fountain), discovered by Emperor Matthias in 1615, for which the palace is named. There is even a famous zoo founded by Maria Theresa's husband, Franz I, in 1752. The prince's former mews are now occupied by the Wagenburg Museum, where the imperial coaches are on view alongside other historical modes of transport such as sedan chairs and sledges.
Open: guided tours April to October 08.30–17.00 hrs; November to March 08.30–16.30 hrs. The Gloriette may be visited daily May to October 09.00–18.00. The park is open daily 06.00–dusk. The Wagenburg collection is open May to September Tuesday to Sunday 09.00–18.00 hrs; November to March 10.00–16.00 hrs; April and October 09.00–17.00 hrs. Subway U4.

◆
SCHUBERT MUSEUM
Nussdorferstrasse 54
The birthplace of Franz Schubert in 1797, this Ninth District house has been carefully restored to its original state, and contains a small museum of the composer's effects, portraits and manuscripts. Schuberts's short life ended 31 years later at Kettenbückengasse 6 in the Fourth District. (Also open to public at the same times.)
Open : Tuesday to Sunday 09.00–12.15 hrs and 13.00–16.30 hrs.

◆
ST MARXER FRIEDHOF
Leberstrasse 6
A pilgrimage of interest to Mozart fans. The great composer died a pauper in 1791, and is buried here in St Marx's Cemetery.
Open: April to September 07.00–18.00 hrs; May to August 07.00–19.00 hrs; October 07.00–17.00 hrs; November to March 09.00 hrs–dusk.

Excursions

◆◆
BADEN
18 miles (30km) south of Vienna
The Romans were the first to appreciate the healing qualities of Baden's 15 medicinal springs, but it was Franz I's imperial patronage which transformed the town into a fashionable society retreat during the 19th century. The nobility arrived by the coach-load to take the waters and build summer villas around the area. Mozart, Schubert and Liszt were frequent visitors, and Beethoven

WHAT TO SEE

completed his *Ninth Symphony* here. The focal point of the town is the **Kurpark**, where a dip in the sulphurous waters (which reach a top temperature of 94°F/35°C) is recommended for the relief of rheumatic and intestinal complaints. Like most spa towns, Baden has a casino to while away the time, and the centre of town is pedestrianised.

◆◆◆
DÜRNSTEIN
40 miles (64km) west of Vienna
One of the most enchanting small towns along this picturesque stretch of the Danube, known as the 'Wachau', Dürnstein is a favourite stopping point for cruises upriver from Krems. The town was famous for its medieval castle, the **Kuenringerburg**, built by the piratical Kuenringer lords, who made a living demanding money with considerable menace from unwary river traffic. Richard the Lionheart (Löwenherz) was imprisoned in the castle by Duke Leopold V during the winter of 1192, before being handed over to Emperor Heinrich VI and ransomed for an enormous sum which financed a new city wall around Wiener Neustadt and an expedition to Sicily. You can explore the ruins of the castle, largely destroyed by the Swedes in 1645, which still dominates the walled town; or

Dürnstein's castle, once a prison for travellers, now attracts them

head for the brightly-painted former abbey church with its handsomely carved wooden door. The narrow main street runs parallel to the river, lined with shop signs, ancient houses and comfortable cafés. Dürnstein's wine-presses pour out vast quantities of refreshing Heuriger wine, or you can sample the deceptively delicious locally-brewed apricot schnapps.

◆
EISENSTADT
28 miles (45km) south of Vienna
Capital of the Burgenland province, Eisenstadt is still a small town chiefly noted for its connection with the composer, Joseph Haydn. Haydn lived here from 1762–90, under the patronage of the Hungarian aristocrat, Prince Nikolaus Esterhazy. You can visit several rooms and galleries in the 17th-century Esterhazy Palace, including the Great Hall where Haydn performed for the prince's court. The composer lived at Haydngasse 21, which now contains a small museum with additional rooms commemorating Listz, and dancer Fanny Elsser. Haydn's tomb can be seen in the local parish church. The road east, from Eisenstadt towards Neusiedl, is known as the **Weinstrasse**. It is lined with wine cellars and roadside stalls selling wine and local produce.

◆◆
KLOSTERNEUBURG
7½ miles (12km) northwest of Vienna
On the edge of the Vienna Woods, this Augustinian abbey is said to have been founded by the Babenberg Duke Leopold III on the spot where his bride's veil was retrieved in 1106. The original Romanesque buildings have been extensively altered, and what you see today is largely the 18th-century work undertaken for Karl VI, who planned to create a rival to Philip II's Escorial palace near Madrid. His plan for a massive baroque church-cum-palace with four spacious courtyards and nine domes each topped with a Habsburg crown was started in 1730 to designs by Donato Felice d'Allio. But building work stopped on the emperor's death in 1740, and only two of the domes were ever completed – those of the empire and the Austrian archduchy. The grandest baroque feature is the Leopoldskapelle, which has a lovely Gothic cloister, and contains the remarkable 1181 Verdun altar, composed of 51 enamelled panels depicting scenes from the Bible. A tour of the monastic buildings includes the Imperial Apartment, the Tapestry Room and grandiose Marble Hall, plus there is a museum and the wine vaults.

◆◆
KREMS
36 miles (58km) west of Vienna
At the heart of the region's wine producing area, Krems is a medieval tree-shaded town on the Danube, peaceful but for the merry clink of glasses emanating from the courtyard inns along Obere Landstrasse. Take a walk through the 15th-century Steiner Tor gateway,

Melk's astounding abbey

and head for the
Dominikanerkirche off
Pfarrplatz. This former
Dominican church has been
converted into a medieval art
museum with frescos by
Kremser Schmidt, altar paintings
by Franz Anton Maulbertsch,
carvings, furniture and metal-
work. On the oldest square,
Hoher Markt, stands the Gothic,
arcaded Gozzoburg, built in the
13th century.

◆◆◆
MELK
48 miles (76km) west of Vienna
Famous for its fabulous
Benedictine abbey, Melk nestles
in a bend of the Danube at the
southern extent of the Wachau.

The enormous orange and white
baroque abbey stretches like an
ocean liner along a promontory
above the river, dwarfing the
town in its lee. Built in the early
18th century, it occupies the site
of a former fortress from which
the Habsburgs' predecessors,
the Babenbergs, first ruled back
in the 10th century. Margrave
Leopold II handed it to the
Benedictines in 1106, then the
fortress was destroyed by fire
and rebuilt in the Gothic style
before finally making way for
Jakob Prandtauer's masterpiece,
started in 1702. The exterior,
with its serried ranks of
windows, is crowned by a pair

of ornate clock towers and an octagonal dome. From the painted Marble Hall, there is access to a terrace with fine views over the river before entering the extensive Library, which houses some 800,000 books, manuscripts and precious documents. The abbey's lavishly gilded church has a high altar by Antonio Beduzzi, who also made the pulpit, choir and confessionals.

◆

PETRONELL

24 miles (38km) east of Vienna
This is a chance for archaeology enthusiasts to visit excavations at the ancient site of *Carnuntum*, capital of Roman Pannonia. In the 2nd century this was a prosperous commercial centre catering for the Roman armies of occupation – thousands of Roman soldiers waiting to prevent a barbarian attack. There are extensive

Trails of the Vienna Woods

ruins, including a Roman amphitheatre that is used as the site of a summer festival, and a museum.

◆

SALMANNSDORF

3½ miles (6km) west of Vienna
This village is one of Austria's oldest. Franz Schubert once lived on Dreimarksteingasse as did Johann Strauss' grandfather. It is a pleasant and popular walk from here to the medieval village of Sievering.

◆◆◆

WIENERWALD

20 miles (32km) west of Vienna
The Vienna Woods cover some 483 square miles (1,250 sq km), much of which was used by the nobility for hunting.
It is a region of villages full of *Heurigen* like
Gumpoldskirchen, one of the prettiest, with quiet wine gardens and a 16th-century town hall; or **Perchtoldsdorf**, a larger but also popular drinking spot. In the wine town of

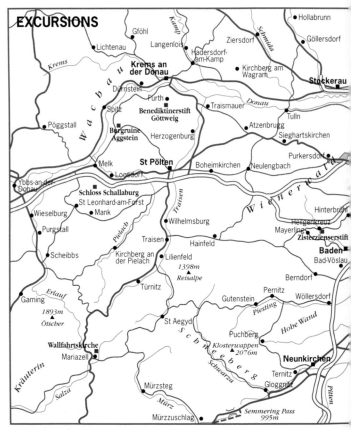

EXCURSIONS

Hollabrunn

Gföhl · Ziersdorf · Göllersdorf

Lichtenau · Langenlois · Hadersdorf-am-Kamp

Krems an der Donau · Kirchberg am Wagram · **Stockerau**

Dürnstein · Fürth · Traismauer · Tulln

Spitz · **Benediktinerstift Göttweig** · Atzenbrugg · Sieghartskirchen

Pöggstall · **Burgruine Aggstein** · Herzogenburg · Purkersdorf

Melk · **St Pölten** · Boheimkirchen · Neulengbach

Ybbs-an-der-Donau · Loosdorf

Schloss Schallaburg · St Leonhard-am-Forst · Hinterbrühl

Wieselburg · **Mank** · Wilhelmsburg · *Wienerwald* · Heiligenkreuz · Mayerling · **Zisterzienserstift**

Purgstall · Traisen · Hainfeld · **Baden** · Bad-Vöslau

Scheibbs · Kirchberg an der Pielach · Lilienfeld · *1398m Reisalpe*

Türnitz · Berndorf

Gaming · *1893m Ötscher* · Pernitz · Gutenstein · Wöllersdorf · *Piesting*

St Aegyd · *S c h* Puchberg · *Hohe Wand*

Wallfahrtskirche Mariazell · *Klosterwappen 2076m* · **Neunkirchen**

Kräuterin · *Salza* · Ternitz · Gloggnitz · *Pitten*

Mürzsteg · *Mürz*

Mürzzuschlag · *Semmering Pass 995m*

Mödling your sightseeing could include the 15th-century Spitalkirche and the house where Beethoven worked on his *Missa Solemnis*. In **Hinterbrühl**, the local inn, converted from an old mill, is said to have been the inspiration for Schubert's song cycle to the miller's daughter, *Die Schöne Mullerin*.

There are two extra special sites in the Wienerwald only 2 miles/3km apart: **Mayerling**, and the Abbey of Heiligenkreuz. In January 1889, Franz Josef's son and heir, Archduke Rudolf, shot himself and his teenage mistress at a remote shooting lodge near the village of Mayerling after his father had refused to annul his unhappy marriage. Enormous efforts were made to conceal the scandal by the government and police. The body of the Archduke's young lover,

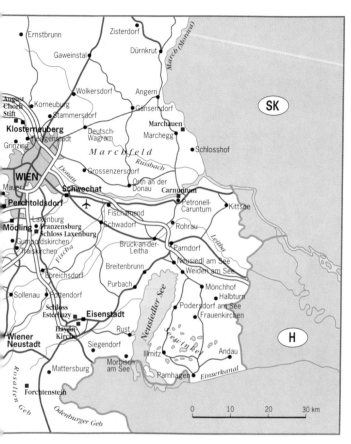

Baroness Mary Vetsera, was
swiftly removed and buried at
Heiligenkreuz; Franz Josef had
the lodge razed to the ground
and replaced by a convent. The
12th-century **Abbey of
Heiligenkreuz** is the most
important of the Babenberg's
religious sanctuaries, founded
by Leopold III in 1133. Its name
means 'Holy Cross' after a
fragment said to be from
Christ's true cross bequeathed

to Austria in the 12th century by
the King of Jerusalem. It is now
kept beneath the high altar of
the Cistercian abbey church.
Giovanni Giuliani designed the
choir stalls inside the basilica,
and also the Trinity Column (or
Pillar of the Plague) which
stands in the courtyard.
Along the basilica's south side,
300 red columns make up the
impressive 13th-century
cloister.

PEACE AND QUIET

Wildlife and Countryside in and around Vienna
by Paul Sterry

Although the landscapes around Vienna and in the province of Burgenland are perhaps Austria's least distinctive, the wildlife here is rich and varied. This diversity is due, in part at least, to Vienna's geographical position. It lies on the doorstep of eastern Europe, and the flora and fauna of the region contain elements from both east and west. Within a day's journey of the city, visitors can find everything from primeval woodlands to alpine pastures. However, Vienna's greatest wildlife attraction lies almost on its doorstep. The Neusiedler See and Seewinkel area have some of the finest wetland habitats in Europe and are a 'must' for the naturalist. There are also relict reminders of what the great Hungarian Plains must have looked like in their prime: a sea of specialised grassland, rich in flowers, birds and insects.

The Schönbrunn Palace Gardens

It is agreeable to find that a cultural and historic attraction (the Schönbrunn Palace is one of the most magnificent sites in Vienna) can also be good for wildlife. Birdwatchers, in particular, will find plenty of variety, and insects and reptiles are also well represented.
The leafy avenues are the haunt of both red-breasted and

Fountain of the Naiads, Schönbrunn

collared flycatchers, with the latter species sometimes breeding in the nest boxes provided. The red-breasted flycatcher is a charming, rather retiring bird, with predominantly grey and buff plumage, but a becoming orange bib. The male collared flycatcher has striking black and white plumage and is altogether bolder. These migrant birds are both most easily seen in spring when the males are singing; by July and August you have to search hard among the foliage to see them.
If you walk past the flower borders up the slope away from the palace, you will come to an area of semi-natural woodland. Year-round residents include red squirrels and birds such as nuthatches and great tits: some individuals may come to food. Hawfinches and middle-spotted woodpeckers can also be seen. Both are accustomed to the presence of man and often reward quiet observers with amazingly good views. Look for large Aesculapian snakes basking in the undergrowth.

Villages

Many of the rural communities in eastern Austria give the strong impression that nothing much has changed in centuries. The pace of life is slow and relaxed and this is reflected in the variety of wildlife – especially birds. Pride of place among the birds must go to the white storks. These are a frequent sight, especially in villages such as Rust and Illmitz, which are situated around the shores of Neusiedler See.

PEACE AND QUIET

White Stork.

With a wingspan of over 5 feet (1½m) and a length of more than 3½ feet (1m), the white stork is one of Europe's largest birds. It is also one of the most distinctive: white plumage and black wings contrast with the bright red legs and bill. Storks are summer visitors to the Vienna area and most nest on buildings. There is a belief that by choosing a particular house to nest on, the birds confer luck on the household, and many houses have old cart wheels or wooden frameworks on their roofs as an inducement to the storks. In the spring, the newly arrived pairs of storks perform elaborate displays by raising their necks and heads and clapping their bills. This behaviour continues, to a lesser extent, throughout the season. The storks of eastern Austria are accustomed to man and are seldom shy.

Neusiedler See

Neusiedler See, which straddles the Austrian-Hungarian border 30 miles (48km) southeast of Vienna, is one of the best wetland areas in Europe. The shallow lake – on average about 3 feet (1m) deep – is 22 miles (35.4km) long and up to 6 miles (9.6km) wide in places and because of the shallowness of the water, almost the entire margin of the Neusiedler See is fringed in immense reed-beds. It has no natural outlet and so, not surprisingly, the water is slightly saline.

Although the reed-beds are a haven for the birds, they can make observation difficult. However, the tracks and roads which lead to the shoreline from Rust, Breitenbrunn, Weiden and Podersdorf-am-See, and especially Illmitz, offer the best opportunities of viewing both reeds and open water.

During the winter months, Neusiedler See and the surrounding land attract vast numbers of wildfowl – over 100,000 in good years – including thousands of white-fronted geese and bean geese. However, spring and summer are probably the most rewarding seasons for the birdwatcher: tens of thousands of birds nest in the area and many more pass through on migration.

Almost any bush or tree around the lake may harbour nesting penduline tits. These engaging little birds build an elegant and intricately constructed flagon-shaped nest suspended out of harm's way from the end of a branch. Outside the breeding season they roam around in flocks of 50 or more birds, attracting attention with their high-pitched calls.

The reed-beds are the haunt of thousands of breeding birds. Several species of herons, bitterns and egrets, as well as spoonbills are common and often seen on dawn or dusk flights to and from their feeding grounds. During late summer, Neusiedler See witnesses what, to many people, is one of the most impressive ornithological sights in Europe: hundreds of thousands of swallows and martins roost in the sanctuary of the reed-beds and the sight and sound at dawn and dusk is truly amazing.

For those willing to brave the onslaught of Neusiedler See's mosquitoes, dawn and dusk is also the time to search for the lake's more secretive birds. It is worth sitting quietly beside any area of mud or open area in the reeds visible from a quiet track. Patient waiting may be rewarded with a view of a spotted crake or perhaps even a little or Baillon's crake. These birds, relatives of coots and moorhens are shy at the best of times; their cryptic plumage, variations of brown mottling for the most part, makes them even more difficult to see against the reeds.

The See is home to a variety of wildfowl in the summer months, as well as to great-crested and black-necked grebes and coots.

Great reed warbler

PEACE AND QUIET

Sand lizards are found on heathland

White-winged black terns – sometimes in sizeable flocks – and Caspian terns also pass through the region and are usually seen over the lake's open water, occasionally with Mediterranean gulls.

The area of open water is sometimes dramatically reduced in the summer by evaporation. Because of the shallow nature of the lake, a period of strong winds can also expose the muddy shoreline to a surprising extent. Whatever the cause, this reveals a rich feeding ground for native and migrant species.

The Seewinkel Area

This area of low-lying land, to the east of Neusiedler See, is dotted with small lakes and the remains of plains grassland which once stretched across the Hungarian border. Some parts have nature reserve status and are a naturalist's delight; those worth visiting include the Oberstinkersee, Zick Lacke, Lange Lacke and Zicksee. Zick Lacke lies to the north of the road from Illmitz to the shores of Neusiedler See. An elevated hide allows good views of the water birds around the lake margins. As well as an astonishing variety of birds to be seen all year round, look out for yellow-bellied toads, which try to breed in the ruts and pools beside the track in springtime. Around the margins of Lange Lacke, evidence of the water's salinity can be seen in the type of vegetation found growing there. Glasswort, sea aster, sea club-rush and saltmarsh grass are normally associated with a marine environment, but thrive in the salt-laden conditions. The water chemistry also suits several species of bird, including spoonbills and avocets. Thousands of waders and terns pass through the region during migration time. The variety is often greatest in the autumn and individual birds often tend to remain feeding for a longer period of time than in spring.

The surrounding grassland hosts species of pasque flower and feather grass more usually associated with the remaining Hungarian plains ('pusztas') or the Russian steppes. Spiked speedwell is also abundant in summer, while wartbiter bush-crickets, field crickets and sand lizards scurry through the vegetation.

The Seewinkel area is the last western European site for the meadow viper, a species with beautiful zig-zag markings along its back and which is on the verge of extinction. In common with all the specialised plants and animals of this steppe habitat, fragmentation and loss of habitat to agriculture is the main reason for its decline.

The Tadten Plain

The flat landscape of the Tadten Plain, southeast of Seewinkel, although now comprising largely agricultural land, still harbours pockets of natural grassland. These are somewhat similar in nature to the fragments left in the Seewinkel area, but cover larger areas. This factor, combined with the open nature of the field systems and comparative lack of disturbance, allows one of

Europe's most magnificent birds – the great bustard – to survive. Despite their large size (rather like a turkey with a long neck), bustards are shy birds and soon abandon an area if it is disturbed by man or if the habitat is altered. More than any other bird, the great bustard depends on open grasslands for its survival. Not surprisingly, it has suffered more than any other as agricultural 'progress' has relentlessly destroyed its environment in both Eastern and Western Europe.

Outside the breeding season, small flocks of bustards can occur anywhere to the south and east of Tadten and Wallern. Drive the network of roads using your car as a hide but do not expect to get close to them: they are keen-sighted and wary and will not tolerate your getting out of the car for a better look. The World Wide Fund for Nature protects a special area of natural grassland for the birds. A hide overlooks this at a safe distance and the area must under no circumstances be viewed any closer.

The open, agricultural fields of the Tadten Plain are good for birds of prey including Montagu's harriers and buzzards. It is also renowned for red-footed falcons – occasionally in small flocks – which visit the area in late summer as they disperse from their Hungarian breeding grounds.

The Einser Canal, which marks the border between Austria and Hungary is especially good for small birds which like scrub and reeds, as well as for herons,

PEACE AND QUIET

egrets and bitterns which feed on the abundant supply of amphibians.

Keep an eye open for black storks and birds of prey soaring over the Hungarian border.

Marchauen Nature Protection Area

Situated near the village of Marchegg on the border between Austria and Czechoslovakia, this reserve comprises some of the most pristine and unspoilt riverine forest left in Europe. Ponds, bogs and oxbow lakes mark former meanders of the River March, which is now both the eastern boundary of the woodland and the national border. Alluvial meadows add to the habitat variety, and the World Wide Fund for Nature owns and protects half the total area, the rest being privately owned.

Marchauen is criss-crossed by a network of trails. Although access to the wet woodland is, therefore, straightforward, visitors during the summer months should come prepared for the onslaught of its mosquitoes. On warm days in July and August, Marchauen must rank as one of the worst places in Europe for these troublesome insects.

One of the first sights to greet the visitor to Marchauen is the colony of white storks, nesting not on buildings but in the trees.

Black storks are also occasionally seen circling overhead but the viewpoint at the Eagle Monument in Marchegg, overlooking the River March and Czechoslovakia, is generally better for observing this species.

The water's surface is often covered with water lilies, which provide shade and a degree of protection for Marchauen's fish, frogs and toads. However, these still fall victim to grey herons and night herons and comprise their basic diet.

Several species of woodpecker can be seen and heard in Marchauen. Most impressive of these is the black woodpecker, a bird the size of a crow, which drills holes in the trunks of ancient trees. Other birds also leave tell-tale signs betraying their presence and activities. For example, look for excavated nests of wasps and bees along the more open rides and in the meadows. This will probably have been the work of honey buzzards, which tend to raid colonies of these insects for their grubs.

Visitors will be relieved to know that not all the insects of Marchauen are as hostile as its mosquitoes. The range of butterflies is great and includes swallowtails, southern festoons, Camberwell beauties, Queen of Spain fritillaries and Hungarian gliders, all of which are as lovely or intriguing as their names imply. These are most easily seen in the flower-rich meadows, which harbour such special species as globe thistle and Deptford pink.

To reach Marchegg, drive northeast from Vienna and then south on route 49; the car park is just beyond the village.

Hohe Wand

The scenery of Hohe Wand Nature Park, which lies about 30 miles (50km) southwest of Vienna near Wiener Neustadt, provides a stunning contrast to the flat landscape and rolling hills which surround the city. The name Hohe Wand or 'High Wall' is an appropriate one: imposing cliffs rise from farmland and meadows to form a forest-clad plateau. The cliffs themselves are dangerous and precipitous and no attempt should be made to climb them. They can be viewed both from their base and from the plateau summit – a road winds its way up to the top – from where spectacular views may be obtained.

The flower-rich meadows at the foot of the cliffs are good for butterflies and moths such as wood whites, Jersey tiger moths and the black-and-yellow day-flying moth. A wealth of grasshoppers, bush-crickets and field crickets can also be found by careful searching. Open clearings on the summit near the cliff edge are like miniature alpine meadows and are good for flowers such as wall germander and marjoram, and insects including alpine grasshoppers and scarce copper and Apollo butterflies. The latter is a large and colourful species that is most easily studied – and photographed – in the late afternoon when individuals often sit on flower heads catching the last rays of the sun.

Chamois

Despite persecution, the chamois is a resident of many upland areas of Austria, including Hohe Wand. Although the rock face is extremely precarious, these elegant creatures (goat-sized relatives of antelopes) have no difficulty negotiating the camber and nimbly leap from ledge to ledge with surprising speed and agility.

An Apollo butterfly

PEACE AND QUIET

The Vienna Woods

To the west of Vienna lie rolling hills cloaked in forests: these are the Vienna Woods, or 'Wienerwald'; always popular as a destination for country walks. Despite their close proximity to the city, the woods hold a good variety of plants, birds and insects, and the Lainzer Tiergarten Nature Protection Area, in particular, has an excellent range of large mammals as well.

The Wienerwald can be reached on the Wiener Höhenstrasse west of Vienna; park at pull-ins beside the road. Beech, oak, elm and maple are the predominant tree species in the woods. Birds abound but are most readily seen in spring when they are singing and calling at the start of the breeding season. Easy to recognise is the golden oriole's

A stream in the Vienna Woods

song, which is a loud, fluty whistle.

During the spring, glades within areas of beech may be brightened with patches of colourful coralroot bittercress. Later in the season other plants, including shade tolerant species such as birdsnest orchid, yellow birdsnest, asarabacca and helleborines can be found by careful searching.

Within the Vienna Woods, the Lainzer Tiergarten Nature Protection Area is a former hunting area which now protects and harbours several larger species of mammals in what is effectively a game park. In addition to the characteristic woodland birds, roe, red and fallow deer and wild boar can be seen from the many trails and paths.

FOOD AND DRINK

Food

There is no doubt about it, the Austrians like to eat well and so can you whether you choose a stand-up snack bar, a local *Beisl* pub, a rustic tavern or a fancy restaurant. The main thing to consider is quantity, for Austrian cuisine does tend to be a little on the heavy side (German with finesse, as someone pointed out) and it is served in truly Teutonic portions. You should also bear in mind that many of the dishes reflect the days of the old Empire – dumplings that were first introduced from Bohemia, goulash from Hungary, stuffed cabbage from Poland, so that what is and what is not an Austrian speciality may have become confused.

If there is one thing that is particularly Viennese, it is the *Wienerschnitzel*. There is hardly a menu in town where you will not find this thin slice of veal dipped in egg and breadcrumbs then sautéed, and, as you know, it has become popular enough to find its way around the world. Traditionally, it is accompanied by cold potato salad or cucumber salad, but you may prefer an alternative side order, like *Geröstete* (sautéed potatoes). The *Wienerbackhendl* (boned roast chicken) is prepared in a similar way. Then there is *Tafelspitz* which was a favourite of Emperor Franz Josef – a substantial Viennese version of boiled beef. And if there is an absolute fixture of Austrian cooking, it has to be *Knödel* (dumplings). They get into everything from soups, perhaps

Loafing around Vienna

FOOD AND DRINK

disguised as *Leberknödel* (liver dumplings), and even desserts, when they are filled with cream cheese and called *Topfenknödel*, or with hot apricot, then known as *Marillenknödel*.

Because Hungary was for so long part of the Habsburg empire, *Goulash* can scarcely be separated from Austrian cuisine, though depending upon the restaurant, its spiciness will vary. It is the perfect 'warmer' for winter weather as is *Debreciner* sausage and the countless thick soups. Fruit soups are also popular, no doubt by way of Hungary, and may be served hot or cold. Roast goose with dumplings and red cabbage was undoubtedly introduced from Poland, but it is a popular dish in Austria, especially at Christmas. Other favourites are *Cevapcici* (meatballs) and *Schaschlik* (kebabs), which were introduced from Yugoslavia. Snacks are also part of

Viennese life. Some butchers shops and fish sellers actually have their own snack bars, or there are the street *Würstelstands* where you can concoct a superior hot dog from a whole variety of sausages – *Frankfurter, Debreziner, Krainer, Burenwürst* – served with mustard and possibly a *Kaiser-semmel* roll. The *Semmel* is as Viennese as Strauss – a little white bread bun that makes a perfect picnic vehicle for your favourite cheeses and cold cuts. While on the subject of bread, do not forget to try some of the *Bauernbrot* or *Landbrot* which is a thick crunchy-crusted dark rye bread, or there is *Vollkorn*, a full kernelled bread that stays fresh for days.

The Viennese have such a sweet tooth that almost everything comes *mit Schlag* (with cream), from the jam-and-nut-filled *Palatschinken*

Sachertorte, Apfelstrudel and Kapuziner: classic café fare

FOOD AND DRINK

pancakes to deliciously flaky *Apfelstrudel*, flavoured with raisins and cinnamon. The range of pies and cakes available knows no end, and there is none more famous than *Sachertorte*, a rich chocolate cake made with apricot jam and served with lashings of whipped cream. It turns up in all kinds of versions, but officially the Sacher Hotel bakes the definitive article.

No visit to Vienna is complete without one blow-out in a *Konditorei* (pastry shop), or a leisurely binge in a *Kaffeehaus* (coffee house), which not only sells cakes and sweetmeats over the counter but provides seating as well.

Coffee itself is a Viennese art form. Ask for a simple *Portion Kaffee* and you will be served black coffee with a jug of warm milk on the side, but at breakfast the locals tend to drink *eine Melange*, a large cup of half coffee, half milk. Order *einen Braunen* and you will be given coffee with a dash of milk, or *Mokka* which comes in a small cup and is very strong and black. If you want a whipped cream topping simply add *mit Schlag* for one scoop, *Doppelschlag* for two, or *einen Einspänner* which is coffee with whipped cream and arrives in a tall glass. Lest you forget, there is always *Türkischer Kaffee* – thick and sweet black coffee from the Balkan region. As it happens, the Austrians can thank the 17th-century Turkish invaders for coffee in the first place. According to popular legend, a few bags of coffee beans captured in the course of

battle furnished Vienna's first coffee house on Domgasse. By Maria Theresa's time, there were numerous coffee houses where it was considered fashionable to spend hours discussing politics or art. The most prominent like the Griensteidl, Café Central and the Herrenhof became the 'in' places for both business and socialising. Others provided a warm and convivial alternative to cold and lonely lodgings. The old-style coffee house does still exist in Vienna, though not in such numbers and though you will pay more dearly for your *Kapuziner* (cappuccino), you are left in peace to enjoy it, unlike the newer, chrome-plated cafés, or stand up espresso bars.

Restaurants are officially starred from one to five. A 5-star establishment is expected to offer exceptional quality and gastronomic excellence, coupled with what the tourist office refers to as 'extraordinary' service, a wine list that is above par and a staff which is multi-lingual. Similarly, a 4-star restaurant's staff is expected to have a good knowledge of the main foreign languages and a menu that features a variety of wines and liquors, plus international specialities as well as local cuisine. Three stars denote 'good quality'; two stars offer 'satisfactory' cuisine; and one star equals 'adequate'. Do keep in mind that during July and August, some restaurants close for their summer holidays, although the best hotel dining rooms are open year-round.

FOOD AND DRINK

Luxury Restaurants

A number of hotels boast elegant restaurants in this category, such as the Hotel Bristol's celebrated Art Nouveau dining room, the **Korso**, which serves some of the finest cuisine in the city. Vienna's top class restaurants generally feature both Austrian specialities and international dishes on their *à la carte* menus but may also include a fixed price or gourmet menu. This is a popular option at the Inter-Continental's **Vier Jahreszeiten** and at the Imperial's **Zur Majestät**. (For details of hotel dining rooms, see Accommodation page 95–97.)

Austrian Speciality Restaurants

At the top of the range, one of the best known, and worthy of the 'luxury' label, is **Zu den 3 Husaren**, Weihburggasse 4 (tel: 512 10 92). Ideally located in the First District, it has a truly Viennese atmosphere and all the dishes you should try. Zither music adds that *gemütlich* touch at **Stadtkrug**, Weihburggasse 3 (tel: 512 79 55); and ask for *Tafelspitz* at **Zum König von Ungarn**, Schulerstrasse 10 (tel: 512 53 19).

Not quite so pricey is rustic **Kupferdachl**, Schottengasse 7 (tel: 5339 38114) which offers classic and light Austrian cuisine. It is a good place to dine before a night at the theatre. At **Restaurant im Mailberger Hof**, Annagasse 7 (tel: 513 40 82), you may dine in the garden in summer. A typically cosy Vienna restaurant with seasonal delicacies is **Serviette**, Wiedner Hauptstrasse 27–29 (tel: 501 11 325); while the **Wiener Rathauskeller**, Rathausplatz 1 (tel: 42 12 10) is probably one of the most traditional in this 5-star bracket, including the music. **Gösser Bräu**, Elisabethstrasse 3 (tel: 587 47 50) is more of a traditional *Bierkeller*, and you can be sure of a good choice of local wine at **Paulusstube**, Walfischgasse 7 (tel: 512 81 36). Ideal if you are spending a night at the opera is **Sirk-Rötisserie**, Kärntnerstrasse 53 (tel: 515 16 552). **Stadtbeisl**, Naglergasse 21 (tel: 533 33 23) is an intimate tavern in the heart of town; **Zum Laterndl**, Landesgerichtsstrasse 12 (tel: 406 43 58) is traditional and locally popular.

Going down the price scale, try **Zum Bettelstudent**, Johannesgasse 12 (tel: 513 20 44); or **Zur Linde und Lindenkeller**, Rotenturmstrasse 12 (tel: 512 21 92).

Eastern European Speciality Restaurants

Good but not cheap Yugoslavian cooking is the key fare at **Dubrovnik**, Am Heumarkt 5 (tel: 713 27 55). For Polish meals try **Polonez**, Wolfgang Schmälzgasse 8 (tel: 218 63 77). Excellent Russian cuisine, but high-priced, is available at **Feuervogel**, Alserbachstrasse 21 (tel: 34 10 392). When it comes to Hungarian, you have plenty of choice, and many of the restaurants provide live music Hungarian-style to go with the goulash. Recommendations include: **Csarda im Hotel Hungaria**, Rennweg 51 (tel: 713 25 21);

FOOD AND DRINK

Mathiaskeller, Maysedergasse 2 (tel: 512 21 67); and **Ungar-Grill**, Burggasse 97 (tel: 93 62 09).

Other Continental Restaurants
Fresh fish prepared French-style is what to order at **Chez Robert**, but it is somewhat out of the way at Gertrudplatz 4 (tel: 43 35 44). **Salut**, on the other hand, also specialises in fish and is centrally located at Wildpret-markt 3 (tel: 533 13 22). Greek restaurants are traditionally easy on the wallet – try **Der Grieche**, Barnabitengasse 5 (tel: 587 74 66); or alternatively **Schwarze Katze**, Girardigasse 6 (tel: 587 06 25).
Pizzerias are plentiful in Vienna, but for first class Italian fare with an emphasis on pasta and fish, **Grotta Azzurra**, Babenbergerstrasse 5 (tel: 586 10 44) is a good bet. There is a rich flavour of Tuscany at **Ristorante Firenze Enoteca**,

Mecca for the sweet-toothed: cakes and pastries are mouthwateringly tempting

Singerstrasse 3 (tel: 513 43 74). Less expensive Italian restaurants include:
Bistro Rebhuhn, Goldschmiedgasse 8 (tel: 533 61 55); **Ristorante Da Gino e Maria**, Rechte Wienzeile 17 (tel: 587 45 70); and **Ristorante da Luciano**, Sigmundsgasse 14 (tel: 523 77 78). A top class, top price Turkish restaurant is the well-known **Kervansaray**, Mahlerstrasse 9 (tel: 512 88 43).

Far Eastern Cuisine
Indian food has proved popular in Vienna, where one of the most exclusive restaurants to offer it is **Demi Tasse**, Prinz-Eugen-Strasse 28 (tel: 504 31 19). Sitar music accompanies the Tandoori and other Indian dishes at **Rani**, Otto-Bauer-Gasse 21 (tel: 56 51 11); and at

FOOD AND DRINK

Taj Mahal, Nussdorferstrasse 38 (tel: 34 51 01). Locals have a preference for **Maharadscha**, Gölsdorfgasse 1/Salzgries 16 (tel: 533 74 43). Cheap but central **Koh-i-noor**, Marc-Aurel-Strasse 8 (tel: 533 00 80) is another winner.

Japanese restaurants are far outnumbered by their Chinese counterparts in the city, but counted among the best is: **Mitsukoshi**, Albertinaplatz 2 (tel: 512 27 07); and **Sushi-Yu**, Ungargasse 6 (tel: 713 89 14).

Vegetarian
Estakost, Währingerstrasse 57 (tel: 42 50 654) is a great place for a vegetarian lunch and has a special menu for diabetics. Wholefoods, large pizzas and salads are the offerings at **Hartberger Ringstuben**, Währingerstrasse 33–35 (tel: 43

Waltz Restaurant on the Blue Danube

33 35); wholefoods also appear on the menu of **Restaurant Burgtheater**, Teinfaltstrasse 8 (tel: 533 55 56). The menu is pretty diverse at **Siddhartha**, Fleischmarkt 16 (tel: 513 11 97), though some would say prices are a bit inflated. **Restaurant Wrenkh** has two locations, both favoured by young vegetarians for their reasonable prices and good wines. The most central address is Bauernmarkt 10 (tel: 533 15 26) with an adjacent café selling hot and cold vegetarian snacks.

Nouvelle Cuisine
The portions may be smaller, but this is rarely reflected in the bill. However, three recommendations aimed at the younger market are: **Hedrich**,

Stubenring 2 (tel: 512 95 88), which may resemble a snack bar, but is always crowded and does feature excellent cuisine. One charming small restaurant with handwritten menus and a good stock of wines is **Der Pfiff Um Die Ecke**, Wilhelm-Exner-Gasse 23 (tel: 341 03 42). Somewhat out of the central district, **Peter's Beisl**, Arnethgasse 98 (tel: 46 53 75), is a typical tavern by day but becomes a nouvelle cuisine restaurant at night.

Quick and Inexpensive

Recommended **Naschmarkt** snack bars are located at: Schottengasse 1; Schwarzenbergplatz 16; and Mariahilfer Strasse 85. The **Chattanooga-Snackbar**, Graben 29a, is also first class. The **Nordsee** chain appears at the following locations: Kohlmarkt 6; Naschmarkt; Mariahilfer Strasse 34 and 84. A great place for an open sandwich is centrally-located **Duran & Co**, Rotenturmstrasse 11; or **Schwarzes Kameel**, Bognergasse 5, which is a snack bar-cum-deli. One of the most classic Viennese snackbars is **Trzesniewski**, Dorotheergasse 1, or in the Shopping Center Nord-Ignaz-Köck-Strasse where you can wash down your choice of fare with draught beer and thirst-quenching cider (*Apfelmost*). On a more prosaic level, there are recommended cafeterias at Führichgasse 10; Universitätsstrsasse 7; and Ebendorferstrasse 8. For less adventurous fast food addicts, the ubiquitous **McDonalds** is all over the place,

with three central locations at: Schwarzenbergstrasse 17; Johannesgasse 3; and Schwedenplatz 3–4. **Pizza-Paradies** is one of the biggest pizza parlour chains, but the two most centrally-placed, recommended establishments for pizza are: **Pizzeria-Restaurant Adriatic**, Habsburgergasse 6-8 (tel: 533 50 04); and **Pizzeria Grenadier**, Kärntnerstrasse 41 (tel: 51 27 794).

(See also **Beisls**, page 88).

Boat Restaurants

If you feel in the mood for a waltz at tea time (lunch or dinner, too, for that matter) whisk those dancing feet off to the **DDS Johann Strauss**, moored at Schwedenplatz-Kleine Donau (tel: 533 93 67).

Coffee Houses

The traditional Viennese meeting places, where you can sit for hours with a newspaper (almost all the authentic coffee houses carry international newspapers), chat, play chess or even billiards. The following are the most celebrated: **Bräunerhof**, Stallburggasse 2, is a lovely old coffee house popular with young patrons. Plenty of newspapers, plus waltz and operetta music on weekend afternoons. **Demel**, Kohlmarkt 14, should not be missed if only for the aroma. It is almost always crowded and popular with tourists. **Hawelka**, Dorotheergasse 6, is an historic rendezvous for artists, antique dealers and writers. **Landtmann**, Dr Karl-Lueger-Ring 4, belongs to the elite circle of Ringstrasse cafés where it is a must to be

FOOD AND DRINK

seen. **Café Museum**, Friedrichstrasse 6, is an old, much loved and atmospheric coffee house decorated by Adolf Loos, where chess is a serious game. Piano music adds a note of gaiety at **Prückel**, Stubenring 24. **Sperl**, Gumpendorfer Strasse 11, has been renovated into a showpiece with marble tables, Jugendstil chairs and loads of newspapers including *The Times*, as well as billiard tables. Another renovated café, dating from the early days of the Ringstrasse is **Schwarzenberg**, Kärntner Ring 17.

Also recommended are: **Central**, Herrengasse 14, a renovated old-style café, located inside Palais Ferstel. Large though it is, **Eiles**, Josefstädter Strasse 2 is cosy enough. **Café Haag**, Schottengasse 2, is especially popular in summer thanks to its lovely garden in the main courtyard of the former Schotten monastery. An extensive menu is available until late at **Hummel**, Josefstädter Strasse 66, which also starts the day with good breakfasts.

Cafes with music

If you feel the tinkling of the ivories in the background further improves the taste of coffee and cake, try any of the following: **Biedermeier**, Landstrasser Hauptstrasse 28; **Cafe Central**, Herrengasse 14; **Cafe Servus**, Mariahilfer Strasse 57–59; **Cafe Hotel Imperial**, Karntner Ring 16; or **Konzertcafe Schwarzenberg**, Karntner Ring 17.

The strains of the violin are the accompaniment at Cafe Schmid-Hansel, Schulgasse 31. Other sweet spots for music include: **Cafe Braunerhof**, Stallburggase 2; **Cafe Dommayer**, Dommayergasse 1; and **Cafe Pruckel**, Stubenring 24.

Konditorei

Among the best tea rooms and pastry shops in town are **Demel**

Demel's sumptuous café

(see above); **Gerstner**, Kärntnerstrasse 15; **Heiner**, Kärntnertrasse 21-23; **Kurcafé-Konditorei im Oberlaaer Stadthaus**, Neuer Markt 16; **Lehmann Louis**, Graben 12 and **Sluka**, Rathausplatz 8.

Ice Cream Parlours
Take your pick from **Alberti**, Praterstrasse 40, where exotic ice cocktails are a speciality; **Benner**, Prager Strasse 37, a little out of the way, but worth it for wonderful sorbets and parfaits; **Callovi**, Tuchlauben 15a; **Frigo**, Dr Karl-Lueger-Platz 2, coupes of fruit and ice cream a speciality; **Kierger**, Ratschkygasse 14, not so central but good ice cream cake; **Molin-Pradel**, Franz-Josefs-Kai

FOOD AND DRINK

17, myriad varieties; **Tichy**, Reumannplatz 13, calls itself a 'palace of ice cream'; lastly **Valcak**, Simmeringer Hauptstrasse 48.

Drink

So you would rather have a beer or a glass of wine? Then head for a *Beisl* or a sign marked *Bierstube* or *Weinstube*. Austrian beer tends to be reasonably strong and is tasty enough if not outstanding – the local brew is Gösser – but Austrians tend to prefer drinking wine. You can get either at any time of day in pubs, bars, even in some coffee houses.

Almost all of the decent wine is white – look for Vienna's own Grinzinger, Nussdorfer, Sieveringer and Neustifter varieties, or slightly sparkling wines from the Danube Valley, such as Kremser, Dürnsteiner or Langenloiser.

Where you drink your wine is up to you, but one splendid tradition, particularly on a summer's evening are the *Heurigen* in the wine growing districts on the outskirts of the city. *Heuriger* literally means 'of the season', and *heuriger Wein* is 'new' or 'young' wine, which retains this particular status until November of the year following the vintage. Producers do not need a licence to sell their new wine on their own premises. They simply set up shop by hanging a pine branch over the door to announce the arrival of the new vintage.

Authentic *Heurigen* may not have kitchens, but allow customers to bring their own food, though most cellars in the popular Wienerwald area provide meals. Accordian music is another distraction thrown in to attract the tourist trade.

Beisls

Once upon a time, there was a *Beisl* on every corner, and these typical Viennese-style taverns are still the place to find a hearty lunch, a litre of beer or jug of wine.

The following are recommended: **Bastei-Beisl**, Stubenbastei 10 (tel : 512 43 19) for its romantic gaslit atmosphere; **Antiquitäten-Keller**, Magdalenenstrasse 32 (tel: 56 69 533) congenial ambience; **Piaristenkeller**, Piaristengasse 45 (tel:42 91 52) – going strong since 1816 complete with zither music; **Urbani-Keller**, Am Hof 12 (tel: 63 91 02).

Particularly noted for food are: **Gasthaus Heidenkummer**, Breitenfeldergasse 18 (tel: 405 91 63) generous portions served in a pleasant tavern with garden; **Gasthaus Reinthaler**, Gluckgasse 5 (tel: 512 33 66) inexpensive hot meals through the day; **Schweizerhaus**, Prater, Strasse des 1 Mai 116 (tel: 218 01 52) famous for roast pork hock and excellent draught beer; **D'Landsknecht**, Porzellangasse 13 (tel: 34 43 48) notable for reasonably priced homemade desserts and pastries; **Zu Den 3 Hacken**, Singerstrasse 28 (tel: 512 58 95) one of the last old taverns in the city centre with a large menu at small prices; **Zur Goldenen Glocke**, Ketten-brückengasse 8 (tel: 587 57 67) Viennese specialities in an atmospheric garden; **Zwölf-Apostel-Keller**, Sonnenfelsgasse 3 (tel: 512 67 77) wide selection of wines in an historic city tavern.

Heurigen

The most famous wine growing district (and therefore the most popular one to find a *Heuriger*), is **Grinzing**, where there are presently about 20 genuine wine taverns, identified by the word *Eigenbau* that shows the wine grower is serving his own wine. Most of the Grinzing *Heurigen* have large gardens, offer food or at least a buffet, both red and white wine, and usually have music.
The following are open year-round: **Bach-Hengl**, Sandgasse 7–9; **Berger Raimund**, Himmelstrasse 29; **Ing Hengl**

Ferdinand, Iglaseegasse 10; **Rockenhauer Otto**, Sandgasse 12.
Seasonal openers (generally Easter to October) include: **Berger Karl**, Himmelstrasse 19; **Maly Hans**, Sandgasse 8; **Murh Karl**, Cobenzlgasse 12; **Ing H Reinprecht**, Cobenzlgasse 22; **Schmidt Hans**, Cobenzlgasse 38.
Locals prefer the districts of **Heiligenstadt** and **Nussdorf** which are less touristy. This area was a favoured summer retreat in Beethoven's day, and the vineyards on Nussberg produce a really good Rheinriesling. Among those *Heurigen* open year-round are: **Diem's Buschenschenke**, Kahlenberger Strasse 1; and

Grinzing's Heurigen are renowned for their distinctive hospitality

FOOD AND DRINK

Ing Mayer Franz, Beethovenhaus, Pfarrplatz 3. Other recommended seasonal possibilities include: **Greiner**, Kahlenbergstrasse 17; **Muth Hans**, Probusgasse 10; **Schubel-Auer**, Kahlenberger Strasse 22; and **Stift Schotten**, Hackhofergasse 17. Few *Heurigen* in this district feature music and some only open on weekends.

Most of the *Heurigen* in the small wine growing district of **Jedlersdorf** are situated along the main street and their patrons tend to be regulars. Most open alternate months, and offer a generous buffet. On Jedlersdorfer Strasse, you will find **Binder Peter**, at No 151; **Fuchs Kurt**, at No 158; **Kaleta**

Traditional **Heuriger** *sign*

Erwin, at No 161; **Lentner Richard**, at No 159; and **Weiser Wilhelm**, at No 166a.

After a day in the Vienna Woods, you might pick a quiet *Heuriger* in the **Mauer** area. **Lainer Eduard**, Dreistandegasse 5, is open year-round, and there are always a couple of pine needles nailed to the doors on Maurer Lange Gasse, where you will find: **Edlmoser Karl** at No 123; **Grausenburger Leopold** at No 101a; **Hofer Helene** at No 29; **Familie Lentz** at No 78; **Lindauer Josef** at No 83; **Familie Neuwirth Christian** at No 18; and **Familie Stadlmann** at No 30.

Many Viennese patronise the charming **Neustift am Walde** district only recently discovered by adventurous visitors. There is a good selection of taverns on Rathstrasse, including the following venues: **Bachmann Franz** at No 4; **Ferschel Erich** at No 30; **Haunold-Pichler** at No 26; **Huber Walter** at No 15; **Rieger Heinz** at No 22; **Wolff** at No 46; and **Zeiler Hans** at No 41.

Vienna's largest wine growing area is **Stammersdorf** where more than 100 growers produce about a third of the city's wine. Stammersdorfer Strasse is a good place to start, and among those with music on weekends most of the year are: **Ing Eisenheld Karl** at No 81; **Feitzinger** at No 115; **Gstaltner Andreas** at No 21; **Helm Robert** at No 121; **Reichl Franz** at No 41; **Sammer Leopoldine** at No 87; **Schmidt Josef** at No 105; and **Urban Wilhelm** at No 123.

SHOPPING

Catching a coffee between shops

Shopping in Vienna is not cheap but it is elegant. You can be assured that quality goods are of the finest, that presentation is excellent and that service is courteous. Vienna's top stores are found on Kärntnerstrasse, Mariahilfer Strasse, Graben and Kohlmarkt, but if you are looking for a bargain, you might be lucky at the Saturday morning flea market attached to Naschmarkt. Serious antique shoppers will find a heavy concentration of antique shops in the capital.

Small emporiums in the Innere Stadt around Josefsplatz, stock plenty of *objets d'art* and furniture from the old Empire, such as Biedermeier furniture and Jugendstil art pieces. There are said to be over 230 art

dealers and galleries in the city centre, so it is no wonder that Vienna is considered to be one of the world's great centres of the art trade. Coin and stamp collectors could be in luck as well.

Although bargain antique hunting generally requires quite a bit of knowledge, one good place to have a go is the public auction house on Dorotheergasse. The **Dorotheum** was founded by Joseph I in 1707 as a kind of pawn shop for the 'new poor'. Distressed gentlefolk could release cash over the counter in exchange for their heirlooms and redeem them later if times proved more prosperous. It also acted as a clearing house for stolen goods where robbery

SHOPPING

victims could buy back their stolen property if the police had not managed to apprehend the villain and retrieve the loot. Nowadays, goods are displayed prior to a sale and are bid for. If you are not confident enough to bid, a small fee will pay for a licensed agent to do so on your behalf. Buying items at the Dorotheum is not restricted to auction times, you can purchase almost everything over the counter as in a normal store and there are frequent special offers. The Dorotheum main building is at Dorotheergasse 17, plus there are 15 other branches.

Austrian national costume – the traditional low-cut white blouse, apron and full dirndl skirt for women, lederhosen and jaunty hats for men – has its fans, particularly those visitors buying gifts for children, while heavy woollen loden cloth (usually green) makes extremely warm coats, cloaks and jackets, either off the peg or bought by the metre. More classic items of clothing are to be found in suede or leather and of course in this nation of skiers, any winter sports apparel and equipment is of first class manufacture. Austrian crystal may well be a temptation, whether in the form of wine glasses or small animal figurines. Hand-decorated china from the Augarten porcelain workshops is also a favourite souvenir, and the company produces a popular line in decorative Lipizzaner horses. For handy non-breakable gifts, keep an eye out for attractive items worked in dainty petit-point, such as cushions and small handbags.

Antiques

The following specialists in antiques may all be found in the Inner City: **Alt Wiener Kunst**, Bräunerstrasse 11; **Beletage**, Mahlerstrasse 15; **D & S Antiquitaten**, Dorotheergasse 13; **Hampe**, Weihburggasse 9; **Hofstatter**, Braunerstrasse 12; **Reisch**, Stallburggasse 4; **Siedler**, Himmelpfortgasse 13–15. You might also like to note that the **Kovacek Glass Gallery**, Stallburggasse 2, specialises in collectors' items from valuable Biedermeier cups to Baccarat paperweights.

Books

Buchandlungen (book shops) thrive in Vienna. The **British Book Shop** is located in Weihburggasse 8 (tel: 512 19 45). A mixture of continental literature, including English, is for sale on the first floor of **Frick**, Graben 27 and in Das Internationale Buch, Trattnerhof 1. One of the best places for maps is **Freytag-Berndt und Artaria**, Kohlmarkt 9, and for art books, look into Wolfrum, Augustinerstrasse 10. If you cannot find an English newspaper, drop into **Shakespeare & Co**, Sterngasse 2.

Fashion

One of the leading shops for furs and leathers is **Valek**, Seilerstätte 16, which claims to be able to suit every pocket and taste. Quality furs are also available at **M Liska**, Kärntnerstrasse 8. A boutique offering Italian styling is **Alexander**, Rauhensteingasse 10. International designer label handbags and other accessories are the elegant key to **Rada**, Kärntnerstrasse 8; fine Italian leather goods are offered by **Alta Moda**, Mariahilfer Strasse 71; chic and exclusive handbags are the speciality at **Nigst**, Neuer Markt 4; and for fashion shoes look no further than **Zak**, Kärntnerstrasse 36. Also for leather goods, there is **Desiree**, Graben 7; **Kreps**, Wollzeile 31; **Popp & Kretschmer**, Kärntnerstrasse 51. Ladies fashion stores worth looking at include: **Cristina Rojik**, Bauernmarkt 2; **Femina 2000**, Stephansplatz 9; **Maldone**, Hoher Markt 8; and **Sonia Rykiel**, Goldschmiedgasse 5. Folklore fashion is featured at **Trachten Just**, Lugeck 7; and if you are looking for loden, try **Eduard Kettner**, Seilergasse 12. Traditional Austrian national costumes can also be found at **Berger**, Habsburgergasse 9; **Collins**, Opernpassage; **Erhart**, Rennweg 43; **Springer**, Habsburgergasse 9; **Wantky Trachten**, Burggasse 89 and other branches; and **Witzky beim Stephansdom**, Stephansplatz 7.

Gifts

Austrian handicrafts, including Michaela Frey enamelled jewellery and accessories can be found at **Österreichische Werkstätten**, Kärntnerstrasse 6; the best crystal is at **Deckenbacher & Blumner**, Kärntnerstrasse 23. Austrian tin soldiers, toys and souvenirs are sold at **Josef Kober**, Graben 14. A great range of sports equipment can be found at **Berco Sport**, Mariahilfer Strasse 1c. Also good for gifts are

Ostermann, Am Hof 5; **Metzger**, Stephansplatz 7; and **Schwarze Grete**, Kärntnerstrasse 12. If you are looking for really exquisite glass tableware, pop into **Lobmeyr**, Kärntnerstrasse 26, which has been producing select glassware since it was founded in 1823. You will find Vienna's famous **Augarten Porcelain Factory** on Stock-im-Eisen-Platz 3–4.

Jewellery

Former supplier to the Imperial Court, **A E Kochert**, Neuer Markt 15, make fine jewellery in their own workshop. A specialist for Swiss watches and 18-carat jewellery is third generation **Wagner**, Kärntnerstrasse 32; another top name is **Haban**, Kärntnerstrasse 2. Also recommended are **Chopard**, Kohlmarkt 16; **Dauber**, Graben 14; **Hammermuller**, Wipplingerstrasse 31; and **Hubner**, Graben 28.

Records

Music lovers will find a wide selection of record shops in the First District and small speciality shops for rare discs in the Sixth District. Hunt for old records in **Teuchtler**, Windmühlgasse 10; and **Rocktiger**, Gumpendorfer Strasse 60 is the place to go if you are a fan of heavy metal music; avant garde and folk music at **Katzenmusik**, Hafnersteig 10; lots of rock, CDs and videos etc at **Meki**, Morzin-Platz/Ecke Salzgries; and an extensive catalogue in all areas is available at **Virgin Megastore**, Mariahilfer Strasse 37–39.

SHOPPING

Second-hand shops

Among those recommended by the Austrian Tourist Office are: **Second-hand Shop**, Judengasse 5 where the emphasis is on nostalgic fashion; similarly (from 1920) at **Boutique Flo**, Schleifmuhlgasse 15. In the 7th District, **HM-Mode**, Lerchenfelder Strasse 94–98 is a good place to browse; also in the 9th District, **Tauschboutique**, Nusdorfer Strasse 57.

Markets

There are some 20 open markets in Vienna, of which the **Naschmarkt**, on Linke Wienzeile, is the largest and most interesting. (*Open*: Monday to Friday 06.00–18.30hrs, Saturday 06.00–13.00hrs.) On a Saturday, the weekly **Flohmarkt** (Flea Market) occupies the southernmost end of the Naschmarkt's territory and is always fun to browse around if you like bric-à-brac. (*Open*: Saturday 08.00–18.00hrs.) Take the U4 to Kettenbrückengasse to get there. Between March and September, there is a weekend **Art and Antiques Market** held by the Donaukanal, near Schwedenplatz. It is worth investigating for the wide variety of paintings, books, antiques and other items for sale. (*Open*: Saturday 14.00–20.00hrs, Sunday 10.00–20.00hrs.)

Elegant and exclusive shopping at Kohlmarkt

ACCOMMODATION

In Vienna, you can take your pick of hotel accommodation not only by the size of your wallet but by style, especially in the luxury bracket where traditional grand hotels, often converted from former palaces, have been joined by a new breed of sleek modern 'palaces'.

If you are in the market for something a touch more modest, look no further than the numerous pensions, which are clean, comfortable and especially reasonable for longer-stay guests. Pensions are usually rather small and owner-managed, in all probability only providing bed and breakfast. Do not expect a restaurant or business facilities and you could find them a bargain. Hotels are officially graded from one to five stars.

Luxury

The newest deluxe hotel is the 205-room **Ana Grand**, Kärntner Ring I (tel: 515 51 60); opposite the Opera House, the 152-room **Hotel Bristol**, Kärntner Ring 1 (tel: 51 51 60) was built in 1894, and preserves a cherished reputation for generous hospitality, discreet service and the fêted Korso Restaurant. On the Ringstrasse, you will find the 5-star **Hotel de France**, Schottenring 3 (tel: 31 36 80) with 190 rooms, just a few minutes' walk from the city's classic sights. The vast 620-room **Wien Hilton**, Am Stadtpark (tel: 71 70 00) offers a parkside location, an excellent à la carte restaurant and the facilities of the City Air Terminal with direct connections to the airport. The

Hotel Imperial, Kärntner Ring 16 (tel: 50 11 00) can boast 162 rooms (including 21 gracious suites) situated in a beautiful former palace near the Opera. Built in 1867 for the Duke of Württemberg, it was transformed into a deluxe hotel in 1873, and is used as the official residence for State Visits. The Empire-style Restaurant Zur Majestät is one of the city's major gourmet establishments. In contrast, the modern glass frontage of the **Inter-Continental Vienna**, Johannesgasse 28 (tel: 71 12 20) makes for marvellously leafy views over the Stadtpark. It is a popular rendezvous with the Viennese, who favour the plush lobby bar, pastry shop and notable restaurant.

Another glass-and-class favourite is the 304-room **Vienna Marriott**, Parkring 12a (tel: 51 51 80). The airy atrium lobby is an unusual feature, and there are excellent facilities including a swimming pool and fitness centre. One of Vienna's oldest baroque palaces, still owned by the Schwarzenberg family, but now operating in part as an hotel is **Im Palais Schwarzenberg**, Schwarzenbergplatz 9 (tel: 798 45 15).

Vienna's only Relais & Château hotel is set in its own park, and the 40 guest rooms, furnished with antiques, afford views of the Belvedere. West of the city centre, at Schönbrunn, you will find the 309-room **Ramada**, Linke Wienzeile/Ullmannstrasse 71 (tel: 85 040). The Scandinavian Airlines **SAS Palais Hotel**, Weihburggasse 32 (tel: 51 51 70) lies off Parkring. Aiming for the business traveller market, it

ACCOMMODATION

offers up-to-date facilities in beautifully restored *belle époch* surroundings. Lastly is the **Sacher**, Philharmonikerstrasse 4 (tel: 51 456), the dowager of Viennese hotels with 116 rooms, ornate rococo decor, immaculate service, an elegant clientele and, of course, oodles of Sachertorte to sweeten the bill. In 5-star establishments, you can expect to pay between 2,000–4,000 Schillings for a single room, and 1,200–3,250 Schillings per person for a twin or double.

Four-star

There are numerous hotels in this bracket. Among those both reasonably sized and centrally located, you will find: **Astoria**, Führichgasse 1 (tel: 51 57 70) near the Opera House, with 108 rooms and a popular restaurant; **Biedermeier**, Landstrasse Hauptstrasse 28 (tel: 71 67 10) is an attractive complex of restored houses with shops and restaurants; **Europa**, Neuer Markt 3 (tel: 51 59 40) with 102 rooms; **Sofitel Hotel Belvedere**, Am Heumarkt 35–37 (tel: 71 61 60) with 211 rooms and a good reputation; **Rathauspark**, Rathausstrasse 17 (tel: 40 41 20) with 117 rooms; and the **Penta**, Ungargasse 60 (tel: 71 17 50) with 342 rooms.

Among the smaller, most centrally located 4-star hotels are: **Am Parkring**, Parkring 12 (tel: 51 48 00) with 64 rooms; **Am Schubertring**, Schubertring 11 (tel: 71 70 20) with 39 rooms; **Am Stephansplatz**, Stephansplatz 9 (tel: 53 40 50) with 62 rooms; **Capricorno**, Schwedenplatz 3 (tel: 533 31 040) with 46 rooms; **K + K Palais Hotel**, Rudolfsplatz 11 (tel: 533 13 53) with 66 rooms; **Parkhotel Schönnbrunn**, Hietzinger Hauptstrasse 10 (tel: 87 804) with 434 rooms; and the **Royal**, Singerstrasse 3 (tel: 515 68) with 81 rooms.

In the 4-star bracket, expect to pay in the region of 900–1,900 Schillings for a single; 600–1,300 Schillings per person for a double or twin.

Three-star

There is an equally excellent choice of 3-star hotels which are within easy reach of the city sights. Among the best located are: **Austria**, Wolfengasse 3 (tel: 51 523) popular, with 46 rooms; **Kärntnerhof**, Grashofgasse 4 (tel: 512 19 23) with 44 rooms; **Post**, Fleischmarkt 24 (tel: 51 58 30) with 107 rooms; **Roter Hahn**, Landstrasse Hauptstrasse 40 (tel: 713 25 680) with 44 rooms; **Schweizerhof**, Bauernmarkt 22 (tel: 533 19 31) with 55 rooms; **Opernring**, Opernring 11 (tel: 587 55 18) with 35 rooms; and **Wandl**, Petersplatz 9 (tel: 53 45 50) with 138 rooms.

In the 3-star range, expect to pay between 500–1,000 Schillings for a single; 400–800 Schillings per person for a double or twin.

One- and Two-star

For cheaper hotels in a good location, try: **Gabriel**, Landstrasse Hauptstrasse 165 (tel: 712 67 54) with 29 rooms; and **Monopol**, Prinz-Eugen-Strasse 68 (tel: 505 85 26), or the **Rathaus**, Lange Gasse 13 (tel: 43 43 02).

One- and 2-star hotels are likely to cost in the region of 300–600 Schillings for a single; 200–500 Schillings per person for a double or twin.

the Fourth, Fifth and Sixth Districts in the side streets off Linke Wienzeile; the Seventh and Eighth Districts along Spittelgasse and Florianigasse; the Inner City around the Old University quarter (Schönlaterngasse/ Bäckerstrasse); and the pedestrianised zone at Seitenstettengasse/Rabensteig, nicknamed the Bermuda Triangle for the nightspots where you can 'disappear' for the evening.

Cabaret
Unlike Paris and Amsterdam, Vienna does not boast a plethora of sequins and showgirls. Some of the younger haunts, such as **Tunnel**, Floriangasse 39 (tel: 42 34 65) feature a type of cabaret and old time Viennese variety may be seen at **Kabarett Simpl**, Wollzeile 36 (tel: 512 47 42). Other suggestions include **Kabarett & Komodie am Naschmarkt**, Linke Wienzeile 4 (tel: 587 22 75) and **Kabarett Niedermair**, Lenaugasse la (tel: 408 44 92). Variety acts are also on the bill at **Spektakel**, Hamburgerstrasse 4 (tel: 587 06 53) and **Kulisse**, Rosensteingasse 39 (tel: 45 38 70).

Cinema
There are several cinemas which screen the latest films in their original language including: **De France**, Schottenring 5 (tel: 317 52 36); **Burg Kino**, Opernring 19 (tel: 587 84 06); and **Top Kino Center**, Rahlgasse 1 (tel: 587 55 57). A number of cinemas also run unconventional or avant garde films, and old classics such as: **Star Kino**, Burggasse 71 (tel: 93 46 83); and **Votiv Kino**,

Währingerstrasse 12 (tel: 317 35 71).

Concerts/ Classical Music
Concert halls are plentiful, but the two main contenders are the opulent **Musikverein**, Karlsplatz 6 (tel: 505 81 90); and the **Konzerthaus**, Lothringerstrasse 20 (tel: 712 12 11) both of which feature performances by the Vienna Philharmonic and Symphony Orchestras as well as other recitals. Music in Vienna is a year-round experience, but the major season runs from September to June, culminating in the Vienna Festival. During summer, concerts are given in numerous venues around the city, including the Rathaus, Schönbrunn and Belvedere. Individual composers are honoured with their own annual festivals, such as Haydn in March and Schubert in November. The vienna Boys Choir can be heard at the Konzerthaus May, June, September and October on Fridays at 15.30 hrs. Tickets can be obtained through hotels or Reiseburo Mondial, Faulmanngasse 4 (tel: 588 04 162).

Discothèques
Vienna claims to have some 35 discos, which are open until around 04.00hrs, the oldest is Atrium, Schwindgasse 1 (tel: 505 35 94); L.A. Disc-Club, Himmelpfortgasse 23 (tel: 513 83 02) occasionally has karaoke; students tend to gravitate towards **Move**, Donaugasse 1 (tel: 43 32 78) which plays music from the 70s onwards. High tech lighting and a fog machine are the pull at **Pl**, Rotgasse 3 (tel: 535 99 95); while Austrian and

ENTERTAINMENT

foreign groups often perform live at **U4**, Schönbrunner Strasse 222 (tel: 85 83 13) a very 'in' disco which also screens music videos. Also popular with the young crowd is **Volksgarten**, Burgring/Heldenplatz (tel: 63 05 18); and **Nachtwerk**, Dr Gonda Gasse 9 (tel: 616 88 80) where there's always a midnight show.

'In' Spots

For the newest music, take yourself to **Kaktus**, Seitenstettengasse 5 (tel: 533 19 38) on a Thursday, Friday or Saturday night, but prepare for the crowds the later it gets (to 04.00 hrs on Saturday). Loud music packs them into the candlelit vaults of **Steh-Achteri**, Sterngasse 3 (tel: 533 67 14) every day of the week until 02.00 hrs and on Saturday to 04.00 hrs. If you'd rather listen to concert music, try **Aera**'s cellar, Gonzangasse 11 (tel: 533 53 14)

or the exclusively classical style at **Santo Spirito**, Kumpfgasse 7 (tel: 512 99 98) near the trendy Stubentor area.

Beer buffs opt for **Krah Krah**, Rabensteig 8 (tel: 533 81 93) which boasts a liquid menu of some 50 brands, while wine drinkers prefer **Alt Wein**, Backerstrasse 9 (tel: 512 52 22). Both are open from late morning 'til well past midnight. There are several popular evening hangouts between Naschmarkt and Spittelberg: you could stay up all night at **Salz und Pfeffer**, Joanelligasse 8 (tel: 586 66 60) or join the smart set at **Schlossgasse 21**, Schlossgasse 21 (tel: 55 07 67), at least until 02.00 hrs. Cabaret takes place nightly at **Spektakel**, Hamburgerstrasse 14 (tel: 587 06 23) while the music varies at **Cafe Terrassinger**, Rechte

Do you hear a waltz?

Advertising a little night life

Wienzeile 27 (tel: 587 22 36). The non-conformers like the lovely courtyard at **Amerlingbeisl**, Stiftgasse 8 (tel: 526 16 60) for sipping drinks and gossiping even though it's some way from the centre, as is **Tunnel**, Floriangasse 39 (tel: 42 34 65) where you can pick your floor for music, cheap food, art and more.

If you've been painting the town red all evening and are ready for breakfast, there are several 'in' spots in the 7th District. **Europa**, Zollergasse 8 (tel: 526 33 83) is one, offering buffet breakfast between 09.00 and 12.00 hrs. Near the university, **Cafe Stein**, Wahringer Strasse 6 (tel: 319 72 41) is a delightful place for breakfast, from 07.00 hrs daily (10.00 hrs Sunday). Sub culture is at its best at **Arena**, Baumgasse 80 (tel: 78 33 39) where the large inner coutyard of a former slaughterhouse is the stage for a variety of happenings. And if you're ready to travel for the way out, try **B.A.C.H.**, Bachgasse 21 (tel: 450 19 70),

the place to party and hear independent music.

Jazz, Blues and Country

Live jazz and blues can be heard at **Jazzland**, Franz-Josefs-Kai 29 (tel: 533 25 75) until 02.00hrs; while there is first class modern jazz at **Jazzspelunke**, Dürergasse 3 (tel: 587 01 26), also until 02.00hrs. Others recommendations are: **Jazzclub Sixth**, Gumpendorferstrasse 9 (tel: 56 87 10) until 04.00 hrs; **Miles Smiles**, Lange Gasse 51 (tel: 42 84 814) until 02.00hrs or 04.00hrs; **Thelonious Monk**, Sonnenfelsgasse 13 (tel: 512 16 31) until 04.00 hrs; and **Roger Engel**, Rabensteig 5 (tel: 535 41 05) until 02.00 hrs.

Suggestions for an evening of country music might include: **Café Verde**, Gardegasse 3 (tel: 93 91 71) until 04.00hrs; **Nashville**, Siebenbrunnengasse 5a (tel: 55 73 89) until 02.00hrs; and **Papa's Tapas**, Schwarzenbergplatz 10 (tel: 505 0311).

ENTERTAINMENT

Latin Music

Although Latin American music is not so popular in this city as some others, you will find feet tapping to the cha-cha beat until around 02.00hrs at: **Arauco**, Krummgasse la (tel: 73 48 532); **America Latina**, Mollardgasse 17 (tel: 597 32 69); **Macondo**, Hamburger Strasse 11 (tel: 56 77 42); and **Rincon Andino**, Münzwardeingasse 2 (tel: 587 61 25).

Opera and Ballet

All the major performances take place with conspicuous ceremony at the **Staatsoper** (State Opera House), Opernring 1 (tel: 514 44/2960). However, first rate opera may also be heard at the **Volksoper**, Währingerstrasse 78 (tel: 514 44/3318; while performances of operetta and ballet are also staged at the **Theater an der Wien**, Linke Wienzeile 6 (tel: 588 30 265).

For an opera programme preview, check with the tourist board or write direct to: Bundestheaterverband, Goethegasse 1, A-1010 Wien, who will advise on how to order and pick up tickets.

Theatre

The leading theatre is the **Burgtheater**, Dr Karl-Lueger-Ring (tel: 514 44 2959); while the **Akademietheater**, Lisztstrasse 1 (tel: 514 44 2959) concentrates on modern drama; as does the **Volkstheater**, Neustiftgasse 1 (tel: 93 27 76). Musicals can be seen at **Raimundtheater**, Wallgasse 18–20 (tel: 59 77 27); and at **Theater an der Wien**, Linke Wienzeile 6 (tel: 588 30 265)

which also stages ballet productions (see **Opera and Ballet**, above).

Other city theatres of note include: **Theater am Schwedenplatz**, Franz-Josefs-Kai 21 (tel: 535 79 14) for drama; **Ateliertheater**, Linke Wienzeile 4 (tel: 587 82 14) for contemporary works; **Theater Brett**, Münzwardeingasse 2 (tel: 587 06 63) concentrates on mime; **Theater am Auersperg**, Auerspergstrasse 17 (tel: 406 07 07) stages popular works and new plays; while **Theater in der Josefstädt**, Josefstädter Strasse 26 (tel: 402 51 27) dishes up light drama performances and Viennese classics.

There are really only two English language theatres: Vienna's **English Language Theatre**, Josefsgasse 12 (tel: 402 12 60) where favourite old film and theatre stars are likely to appear; and the **International Theatre**, Porzellangasse/Ecke Müllnergasse (tel: 319 62 72), featuring productions of work by English language dramatists. **Open air theatre** takes place between May and September. Firm favourites are the animated revues in the garden of an old Viennese inn, **Hernalser Stadttheater**, Geblergasse 50 (tel: 43 35 43); 19th-century folk theatre at the **Original Wiener Stegreifbuhne**, Maroltingergasse 43 (tel: 92 46 05); and classic Austrian plays plus contemporary drama set against the background of the Biedermeier quarter at the **Jura Soyfer-Theater im Orpheum Donaustadt**, Steigenteschgasse 94b (tel: 93 24 58).

WEATHER AND WHEN TO GO

Vienna's continental climate allows for plenty of variety, with average summer temperatures in the 70°Fs (20–26°C), though it can be hot and sticky during July and August with temperatures rising to above 86°F (30°C). Winter weather is chilly and wet around 32°F (0°C), with the probability of heavy snowfalls between December and February. The most gentle months (warm without being wet) are May, June and September. Travel in April or October and you could be in for any kind of sudden surprise. Bear in mind the city's weather extremes when packing and remember there can be a nippy wind at almost any time. Cover contingencies and take a cardigan or jacket even in summer; in winter, you will need boots, gloves and all the other paraphernalia for keeping wrapped up when out on the streets. Although for the most part, casual attire is perfectly appropriate, the Viennese do dress up for the theatre and opera, so these occasions are well suited to cocktail wear.

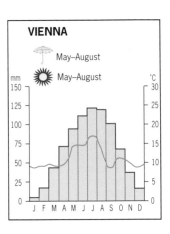

HOW TO BE A LOCAL

The Viennese are nostalgic. They cling on to *Fiakers* (though would not dream of riding in one); throw glittering winter balls in former Imperial palaces; and rub visitors' noses in the gilt of their cultural heritage. Archaic courtly gestures, such as heel-clicking and hand-kissing, have never quite gone out of fashion. Greetings are important: 'good morning', 'good evening' etc, are always used – to strangers as much as to friends. Handshakes are important too. National costume, generally reserved for high days and holidays abroad, can still be seen parading down Kärntnerstrasse in the form of loden capes and hunting hats spiked with feathers. This is all important to know if you want to be a local. Do NOT faint if a chap in a loden coat with a pheasant tail protruding from his head snaps to attention in front of you, clicks his heels and kisses your hand (or shakes it, depending on gender). You could try it, too.

If you are an opera buff, concert goer, classical musician or musicologist, you have an instant entrée to Viennese society. Do not hesitate to use it. In the interval at the Staatsoper or Musikverein, seated in a coffee house or drinking at a trestle table in the local *Heuriger*, you can make instant friends and influence people with your knowledge and appreciation of Vienna's significant role in nurturing great creative talents from Beethoven and Gluck to Bruckner and Mahler.

Viennese humour is pragmatic. They do not, on the whole, find themselves very funny, and for a city where a full quarter of the population is over retirement age, it is not perhaps surprising that they hold some deeply entrenched reactionary views. What is surpuising is that a significant proportion of the youth population share them. Do not attempt to dicuss contentious issues with newfound friends. Vienna now sports several chic glass-and-chrome coffee houses. These are for the young and on the move. In the traditional variety, it is possible to spend an entire day reading the paper, making a couple of telephone calls, catching up on mail and friends. They act as a home from home for the locals, and you will soon blend into the scenery. Driving is something of a liability in the city centre, and you will be better off sticking to public transport with the Viennese. If you do not want to brave the snow on your way out to dinner in the evening, radio taxis are relatively cheap and swiftly summoned. Remember, Viennese restaurants serve dinner between 18.00–21.00hrs. It is rare to find hot food served after 22.00hrs, and most restaurants are closed by 23.00hrs. This is when night owls move on to the 'In' Spots mentioned in the **Entertainment** section (See page 100).

CHILDREN

Though Vienna is largely a concentration of indoor attractions, there are several wide open spaces where children can be let off the leash and allowed to exercise their lungs. There are shows and museums, too. For rainy days and bribery ('You *will* enjoy trailing around another Habsburg palace'), nothing beats a visit to one of the city's calorific pastry shops or the ice cream parlours around Schwedenplatz. (See pages 86/7).

Babysitting Services
The Austrian National Tourist Office guide to *Hotels in Austria* lists hotels with daytime baby-sitting services and facilities. Check directly with the hotel if it offers an evening babysitting or listening service. For daytime babysitters try the Österreichischer Akademischer Gästedienst (tel: 587 35 25) or Österreichischer Hochschülerschaft (tel: 408 70 4675).

Museums
The variety of museums in Vienna should please all ages. Do not miss the **Planetarium** at Prater, on Hauptallee, by the Ferris Wheel. (Closed throughout August.) Two other visits geared towards children are: the **Doll and Toy Museum**, Schulhof 4 (*open*: Tuesday to Sunday 10.00 to 18.00hrs); and the **Circus and Clown Museum** at Karmelitergasse 9, with a great collection of costumes, masks and models (*open*: Wednesday 17.30 to 19.00hrs, Saturday 14.30 to 17.00hrs and Sunday 10.00 to 12.00hrs).

Parks and Zoos

Number one attraction is the
Prater amusement park, full of
year-round, non-stop carnival
action and accessible by
Subway U1. In addition to its
world-famous landmark, the
Riesenrad (giant Ferris Wheel)
built in 1897, the fairgrounds
feature rollercoasters, pinball
machines, carousels and
shooting ranges, plus special
events and festivals. It makes for
a great day out for all the family;
older children will love the
nighttime lights and
atmosphere, too.

Next to the amusement park,
the **Wiener Prater** is an
enormous area of meadows,
wetland forests and small ponds

*Civic parks such as the Rathaus
Garden are popular with children*

CHILDREN

A Fiaker *could bowl you over*

offering pleasant walks, and criss-crossed by bike paths. Tram N takes you through this area along the main Prater Avenue. **Lainzer Tiergarten**, near the former imperial hunting lodge, Hermes Villa, is an enormous game reserve where wild boar roam freely and large enclosures house different species of deer, wild horses, moufflon and aurochs. (*Open*: Palm Sunday to early November Wednesday to Sunday 08.00–dusk; and in winter from 09.00–16.00hrs.) The entrance is situated at Lainzer Tor.

The beauties of Schönbrunn Palace may be lost on the very young, but you can make a compromise. After the palace tour take the youngsters to the zoo in the grounds. (*Open*: in summer from 09.00–18.30hrs; in winter to 16.30hrs.)

Theatres and Shows

How much children will appreciate a performance by the **Vienna Boys' Choir** (see page 21) will depend on their tastes, but it is a pretty safe bet that they will enjoy the **Spanish Riding School** show where uniformed riders put the famous white Lipizzaner horses through their paces. The main performances are held on Sundays for which tickets are quite difficult to come by, but children will be just as enamoured of the Saturday dress rehearsals and the weekday morning workout sessions. (For full details of the school, see page 49.)

No one needs to speak the language to enjoy mime. The **Serapionstheater**, Taborstrasse (tel: 24 55 62) has earned a worldwide reputation for its theatre of pantomime and use of phantasmagorical sets. Puppet shows have international appeal too. Try the Puppentheater Lilarium, Phillipsgasse 8 (tel: 89 421 03). Alternatively, **Theater der Jugend**, Neubaugasse 38 (tel: 521 100) is specifically a theatre for the young and should appeal to teenagers as well. With access to three stages, its repertoire includes slapstick and rock-and-roll productions.

Watersports

On the Alte Donau (Old Danube), there are eight miles (12km) of beaches with bathing areas, five free swimming areas, and boat hire. On Danube Island, it is possible to surf, sail and water ski or chute down the long slide into the water.

TIGHT BUDGET

Accommodation

Camping. There are several campsites on the outskirts of Vienna. For details of campsites, see **Directory**, page 111–112; or contact the Tourist Office (see page 123).

Family Stay. Budget accommodation in a family house. Monthly family stays can be arranged by Mitwohnzentrale, Laudongasse 7 (tel: 402 60 61) (*open*: Monday–Friday 10.00–14.00 hrs and 15.00–18.00 hrs).

Pensions and Small Hotels. The Tourist Office accommodation list covers all price brackets from deluxe to modest 1-star pensions.

Youth Hostels. Open year-round, Vienna's two largest hostels are: Hütteldorf-Hacking, Schlossberggasse 8 (tel: 87 70 263); and Kolpinghaus Meidling, Bendlgasse 10–12 (tel: 83 54 87). For further details, contact: Austrian Youth Hostels Association, Gonzagagasse 22, A-1010 Vienna.

Eating and Drinking

Beisls. Hearty Austrian fare and great value-for-money midday specials are the order of the day at these traditional taverns.

Wurstelstand. Vienna's answer to frankfurter stands are dotted around the city and offer a selection of low cost boiled and grilled sausages with rolls or fries.

Student cafeterias. Those on a tight budget can eat cheaply at these cafeteria even without a student ID. Among those recommended can be found at the New University, Music Academy, Academy of Fine Arts and Academy of Applied Art – all in the 1st District.

Entertainment

Nightlife. It is best to keep to the traditional haunts around the Bermuda Triangle quarter of the Innere Stadt, and the streets off Wienzeile.

Shopping. Shoppers on a budget can bargain hunt at the Saturday flea market at the southern end of Naschmarkt. Record collectors may strike gold browsing around the second-hand shops in the First and Sixth Districts. (See **Shopping**, page 93–94.)

Tickets. Almost all theatres offer student discounts of around 20 per cent on standing room or just pre-curtain call tickets, but not the Vienna State Opera. (See **Entertainment**, page 102.) Discounted tickets to cultural events are sometimes available from the Cultural Section of the Österreichische Hochschulerschaft, Universitätsstrasse 7 (tel: 42 76 11).

Transport

Bicycles. One good way to get around the sights in summer is a bicycle tour led by a guide from Vienna Bike. Details from the Tourist Office (or tel: 319 12 58).

Nightbuses. Save a late night taxi fare on a Friday or Saturday by catching a nightbus. They all depart from Schwedenplatz, and cover various routes throughout the city.

Rides-Riders Wanted Centre. Franzensgasse (tel: 56 41 74) is a great way to cut the cost on trips out of town. The agency matches private car owners with travelling companions to share costs.

24-Stunden-Netzkarte. Do not forget the 24-hour one-price

SPECIAL EVENTS

rover card which gives access to the city's entire public transport network. (See **Directory**, page 120–121.) **Vienna Guides**. Students can get a special half-price deal on off-the-beaten-track tours with Vienna's official tour guides. Brochures are obtainable from tourist offices, the Town Hall, museums and hotels.

SPECIAL EVENTS

January and February
The Fasching Carnival season runs from New Year's Eve to Shrove Tuesday, generating a stream of glittering balls starting with the New Year's Eve Imperial Ball held at the Hofburg, and culminating in the Opera Ball attended by the Austrian President.

March
The Haydn Festival kicks off events on the music front, while there is entertainment for movie buffs at the Vienna Film Festival. The Spanish Riding School begins its spring programme; and the Vienna Marathon is held at the end of March or early April.

April
Spring is in the air judging by the eye-catching flower displays in the Burggarten; and there is a Spring Festival at the Prater.

May
From the middle of the month, the Festival of Vienna attracts an international cast of musicians and theatre groups, choirs and artists, classical and contemporary, who perform night and day for five weeks. Plenty of sideshows and amusements counter the culture blast.

June
The Festival of Vienna is still in full swing, and the Prater celebrates with a colourful Flower Festival. June also marks the first of the Dorotheum's three major annual art auctions (also November and December).

July and August
The summer months find Vienna in the throes of the official music season. The Music Festival complements the numerous concerts and performances with a range of lectures and courses.

September
The Spanish Riding School and Vienna Boy's Choir are back on parade after the summer break. It is also the start of the opera season; and there is plenty of activity at the Autumn Trade Fair.

October
Theatre is in the spotlight this month, with preview tickets selling like hot cakes.

November
Plenty of visitors gather in the city to celebrate Vienna's Schubert Festival. There is an Antiques Fair; and the Dorotheum's November auction.

December
If you didn't pick up any Christmas presents at the Dorotheum in November, there is another chance this month. Also, Vienna is renowned for its wonderful 'Advent in Vienna' Christmas markets on Rathausplatz, on Spittelberg, and at Freyung.

SPORT

Aerobics. Fit & Fun, Landstrasser Hauptstrasse 2a; or John Harris, Nibelungengasse 7.

Bicycling. There are over 178 miles (250km) of marked bike paths in Vienna, which is a cyclist's city. Several pensions are friendly to bikers, offering them secure parking and information. Except on the U6, you may transport bikes on the subway at certain hours of the day. There is a specially marked car, and it costs a half price ticket for the bike. You can also use the Schnellbahn (bikes free on Sundays and holidays). Favourite bike routes will take you to the Hauptallee in the Prater; Danube Island via the Reichsbrücke; Lobau and Laaer Berg. Situated on the Danube, Vienna is a pit stop along the Danube bike route which leads from Passau to Hainburg, southeast of the city. Cycles may be rented at a number of outlets.

Boating. Boats are available for hire on the Old Danube, including sail boats and surf boards. Sailing information may be obtained from the Austrian Yacht Club, Prinz-Eugen-Strasse 12.

Bowling. There is a huge bowling alley in the Prater at Hauptallee 124; and another at Schumanngasse 107.

Golf. Try Golfplatz, Freudenaustrasse 65a; or Golf Wien-Sud, Anton-Freunschlag-Gasse 34–52, out in the 23rd District.

Horse racing. Check out the race courses at Rennbahnstrasse 65 (the Freudenau) for flat racing and steeplechasing; there are trotting races year-round at Prater-Krieau (the Krieau).

Horse riding. This is possible in the Freudenau area of the Prater, where there is a riding centre. Another riding school is located at Barmherzigengasse 17.

Ice Skating. Any time of year you can skate in the Wiener Stadthalle, Vogelweidplatz 14.

Squash. There is a squash club at Heiligenstädter Strasse 82–92.

Swimming. There are several free swimming areas along the Old Danube as well as on Danube Island. Indoor pools can be found at Rogners Margaretenbad, Strohbachgasse 7–9; Amalienbad, Reumannplatz 9; and Jörgerbad, Jörgerstrasse 42. Out in the 10th District, there is an outdoor pool at Kongressbad, Julius-Meinl-Gasse 7. Maybe there is time, too, for a thermal experience at Thermalbad Oberlaa, Kurbadstrasse 14, where you can swim from an indoor pool to an outdoor one.

Tennis. Numerous public tennis courts can be found in the Prater at Rustenschacher Allee; also in Donau Park, Kratochwjlestrasse and Eiswerkstrasse.

People are drawn to Vienna

DIRECTORY

Arriving

Entry Formalities British and North American nationals need only a valid passport to enter Austria for visits of up to three months. Visas are not necessary and neither are inoculations. Vienna's Schwechat International Airport is situated 12 miles (19km) from the city centre (a 30-minute ride), and also handles domestic flights. The modern building offers banking, restaurant, bar and shopping facilities, plus a tourist information office in the Arrivals Hall. Airlines offering direct services from the UK include British Airways and Austrian Airlines.

Austrian Airlines have offices in the UK and the US.

UK 50 Conduit Street, London W1R ONP (tel: (0171) 439 0741).

US Fifth Floor, 608 Fifth Avenue, New York, NY 10020 (tel: (212) 307 6227).

Transport In addition to self-drive cars and metered taxis, there are several public transport services into the city. A regular bus

service operates between the airport and the City Air Terminal (at the Hilton) every 20 minutes from 06.30 to 23.30 hrs and every half-hour from midnight to 06.30 hrs. An additional service connects the airport with both the Westbahnhof and Südbahnhof railway stations running every half-hour between 06.40 and 22.40 hrs; in addition, from April and October trains run between 03.30 and 05.30 every hour. A mini bus shuttle service also operates to hotels and other destinations in the city; seats may be booked when you make airline or hotel reservations, or at the airport itself. Lastly, a train service operates between the airport, Wien Mitte (City Air Terminal), and Wien Nord (Praterstern) every half-hour between 06.11 and 22.16 hrs. Trains take about half an hour, and charge the cheapest fare to the city centre.

Camping
There are five major camping sites on the outskirts of the city. The most central are:

Environment-friendly: a city tram

DIRECTORY

Campingplatz Wien West I,
Hüttelbergstrasse 40, A-1140
Wien (tel: 914 14 49).
Open: mid July to August; three
and a half miles (6km) from city
centre.
Campingplatz Wien West II,
Hüttelbergstrasse 80, A-1140
Wien (tel: 914 23 14).
Open: all year; three and a half
miles (6km) from city centre.
Campingplatz Wien Sud,
Breitenfurter Strasse 269, A-1230
Wien (tel: 86 92 18).
Open: July to August; four miles
(7km) from city centre.
**Donaupark Camping
Klosternenburg**, In der An,
3402 Klosternenburg.
Open: all year; seven miles
(12km) from city centre,
Expresstrain to Vienna.

Car Breakdown
Two auto clubs operate round-
the-clock recovery services. For
assistance, call ÖAMTC,
Schubertring 1-3, A-1010-Wien
(tel: 71 19 90); or ARBÖ,
Mariahilfer Strasse 80, A-1150-
Wien (tel: 891 21).

Car Rental
Avis: Opernring 1 (tel: 58 76
241); or Schwechat Airport (tel:
711 10-2700).
Budget: Wien Hilton (tel: 714 65
65).
Denzel Wolfgang AG
(Europcar): Parkring 12 (tel: 51
55 30); or Schwechat Airport
(tel: 711 10-0).
Hertz: Ungargasse 37 (tel: 713
15 96/0); or Schwechat Airport
(tel: 711 10/2661).
British citizens need only a valid
driving licence to rent a car; US
and Australian citizens need to
apply for an international driving
licence prior to departure.

Chauffeur Services
Chauffeur-driven car rental
services use mainly Volvo or
Mercedes cars. Advance
reservations for renting a car
with an English-speaking
chauffeur can be made through:
Oliva and Posch (tel: 513 38 41);
or Walter Tiller, c/o Vienna
Marriott Hotel (tel: 513 75 05).

Chemists see Pharmacies

Crime
Vienna is a fairly prosperous city,
and the crime and theft rate is
comparatively low. It goes
without saying, however, that you
should not leave valuables lying
around. The police deal quickly
and efficiently with complaints.
Should your passport be stolen,
they will give you a certificate to
take to your consulate.

Customs Regulations
Visitors aged 17 or over arriving
from the EU, US or Canada may
bring the following goods into
Austria duty free: 200 cigarettes
or 50 cigars or 250g of tobacco,
plus a litre of spirits and wine.
There is nothing to pay on
personal jewellery, sports
equipment for personal use or
any gifts brought in to the value
of 400 Austrian Schillings. Nor is
there any restriction on the
amount of foreign or Austrian
currency you bring into the
country.
Leaving the country, you may
export an unlimited amount of
foreign currency and unlimited
Austrian Schillings.

Disabled People
Vienna is reasonably geared up
to accommodate disabled
visitors. Many hotels feature
rooms for the handicapped and

Sit back and see the sights

all the top museums in the city
provide ramps for wheelchairs.
Austrian Airways have a leaflet
on facilities for disabled travellers
at Vienna International Airport;
most of the facilities at the airport
are accessible, including toilets
and the restaurants.
Austrian Federal Railways have
lightweight portable wheelchairs
for use on trains; the chairs must
be booked at least three days in
advance at any railway station in
Austria (no extra cost).

Driving
Vienna's complicated one-way
street system is hard to fathom,
and finding a legal parking spot
is equally difficult.
The Austrians drive on the right,
do not use their horns except in
an emergency, and within the
city the speed limit is 31 miles
(50km) per hour (except 30km

zones). Beware the evening
rush period after 16.00 hrs.
Fuel stations are scattered
throughout the city, some of them
self-service. Most close at night.
If you need fuel very late, try the
highway entrances to the city.
Parking During the winter, you
are not allowed to park on
streets where trams run from
20.00 to 05.00 hrs (exceptions to
the rule are indicated by a
'parking' sign). Where parking
is vetoed, you are allowed a 10-
minute stop.
In parking zones
(*Kurzparkzone*), you may park
between 09.00 and 19.00hrs on
weekdays and 08.00 and
12.00hrs on Saturday, if you
have a valid ticket (maximum
one and a half hours). In districts
6, 7, 8 and 9 a Kurzparkzone will
be introduced in August 1995
with a maximum parking time of
2 hours between 09.00 and
20.00hrs. These are sold at

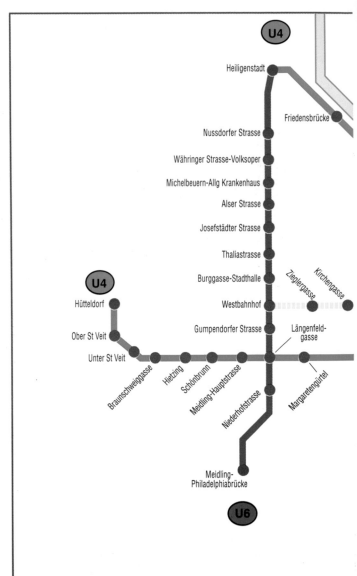

VIENNA : U-BAHN

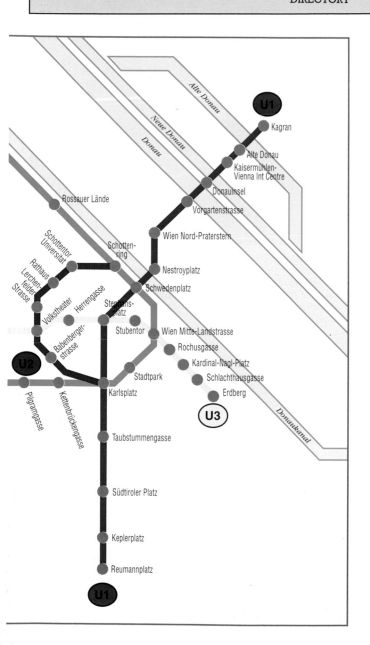

DIRECTORY

Johann Strauss monument

tobacconists, some banks and many fuel stations. There are constant checks by plain-clothes municipal workers who are authorised to extract fines on the spot.
Seatbelts are compulsory.

Electricity
220 volts, 50 cycle AC throughout Austria. Standard Continental two-pin plugs.

Embassies and Consulates
Australia Mattiellistrasse 2–4, 1040-Wien (tel: 512 85 800).
Canada Laurenzerberg 2, 1010-Wien (tel: 531 38 3000).
UK Jauresgasse 10, 1030-Wien (tel: 714 61 17).
US Consulate: Gartenbaupromenade 2, 1010-Wien (tel: 313 39).

Emergency Telephone Numbers
Ambulance (*Krankenwagen*): **144**
Emergency Medical: **141**
Fire (*Feuer*): **122**

Pharmacist: **15 50**
Police (*Polizei*): **133**

Entertainment Information
You will find current listings in the local paper, the free monthly tourist magazine *Vienna Life* and literature available from the Vienna Tourist Board.
Tickets (*Karten*) for entertainment performances may be obtained directly from the venue or from private ticket agencies (*Theaterkartenburo*) and top hotels (although you will pay slightly more for the convenience). You can buy concert and theatre tickets in advance from the **Vienna Ticket Service**, Linke Wienzeile 4, 1060-Wien. However, be prepared for disappointments, as tickets are quickly and regularly sold out.
Österreichischer Bundestheaterverband Bestellburo (National Theatre Ticket Office), Hanuschgasse 3/Goethegasse 1, 1010-Wien (tel: 513 15 13; programme information tel: 514 44 2960)

sells tickets in advance for the Staatsoper (opera), Volksoper (operetta), Burgtheater and Akademietheater (credit cards only). You will need to make reservations for the Sunday performance of the Spanish Riding School and for the Vienna Boys' Choir well in advance of your visit. (For details consult entries in **What to See**.)

Entry Formalities see Arriving

Health

There is an agreement between the UK and Austria to provide British citizens with free in-patient hospital treatment after accidents and emergencies. Other medical services must be paid for, and it is wise to invest in private medical insurance before leaving home. Major hotels should have a doctor on call, or you will find them listed in the yellow pages telephone directory under *Ärztenotdienst*. Hospitals are listed under *Spital*.

Holidays (Public and Religious)

Banks, offices and many restaurants close on public holidays, except for Good Friday, which is a Protestant holiday, when shops remain open.
New Year's Day: 1 January
Epiphany: 6 January
Good Friday, Easter Monday, Ascension Day: variable
Labour Day: 1 May
Whit Monday and Corpus Christi: variable
Assumption: 15 August
National (Flag) Day: 26 October
All Saints' Day: 1 November

Immaculate Conception: 8 December
Christmas Day: 25 December
St Stephen's Day: 26 December

Lost Property

The Lost Property Office (*Zentrales Fundbüro*) is at Wasagasse 22 (tel: 313 44 92 11). Most Viennese are honest and will turn items they have found into the office. Articles left on trams or buses are turned in after three days in the lost property department of Vienna Transport (tel: 79 09/435 00). If you leave something in a taxi, try the Funk-Taxi (radio taxi) numbers; or on a train, (tel: 5800 2996).

Media

The main Austrian newspapers are *Die Presse, Kurier, Neue Kronenzeitung* and *Standard*. English-language newspapers are sold at railway stations and city kiosks, often same-day publications. Books and periodicals can be found at **Das Internationale Buch**, Trattnerhof 1; and **Shakespeare & Co**, Sterngasse 2. There is English-language news on Blue Danube Radio 103.8, at 07.00, 12.00 and 18.00 hrs.

Money Matters

The currency unit is the Austrian Schilling, which is divided into 100 Groschen. Coins are available in denominations of 5, 10, and 50 Groschen and 1, 5, 10 and 20 Schillings. Notes come in denominations of 20, 50, 100, 500, 1,000 and 5,000 Schillings. There are money exchanges (*Wechsel*) open daily at: Schwechat Airport

DIRECTORY

(08.30–23.30 hrs): City Air Terminal (09.00–13.00 hrs and 13.30–18.00 hrs); Westbahnhof (07.00–22.00 hrs); and Südbahnhof (06.30–22.00 hrs). You may also change money in many travel agencies during office hours. Banks are open Monday to Friday 08.00–15.00 hrs (Thursdays until 17.30hrs). Branch offices may close for lunch (12.30–13.30hrs). You will find exchange machines at: Stephansplatz 2, Kartner Strasse 32, 43 and 51, Graben 21, Operngasse 8, Schottenring 1, Schonbrunn Palace, Michaelplatz 3, Tegetthoffstrasse 7 and Franz Josefs Kai 21. The main 24-hour post office, Fleischmarkt 19, will also convert Western European, US and Canadian currencies to schillings. All major credit cards and travellers' cheques are widely accepted in Vienna, but personal cheques will not be accepted unless you have a Eurocheque account.
Now that Austria has joined the EU, you are no longer entitled to a VAT rebate if you are carrying goods out of the country to another European domicile. Non-Europeans, however, may still request a refund when spending more than 1,000 schillings and hand in the U34 form (filled out by the salesperson) to Customs, for stamping, upon departure.

Opening Times
Banks are open Monday to Friday 08.00–15.00hrs (Thursdays until 17.30hrs). Branch offices may close for lunch (12.30–13.30hrs).
Museum opening hours vary considerably, but the main times are Tuesday to Friday 09.00 or 10.00 to 15.00 or 16.00hrs. Saturday and Sunday 09.00–13.00hrs. A few open on Mondays.
Pharmacies are open Monday to Friday 08.00–12.00hrs and 14.00–18.00hrs and Saturdays 08.00–12.00hrs.
Post Offices are open Monday to Friday 08.00–12.00hrs and 14.00–18.00 hrs. Some also open on Saturdays 08.00–10.00hrs. The main post office is open 24 hours.
Shops are generally open Monday to Friday 09.00–18.00hrs and Saturdays 09.00–12.00hrs. Food stores often open as early as 07.00hrs, but then close for lunch 12.30–15.00hrs. The Westbahnhof and Südbahnhof (railway station) shopping arcades are open daily from 07.00 to 23.00hrs.

Pharmacies
A pharmacy or drugstore is known as an *Apotheke*. Normal opening hours are Monday to Friday 08.00–12.00hrs and 14.00–18.00hrs, Saturday 08.00–12.00hrs. All pharmacies display the address of the nearest 24-hour *Apotheke*. You can call an emergency line (tel: 15 50) for advice. There are English-speaking pharmacists at Internationale Apotheke Kärntner Ring 15 (tel: 512 28 25).

Places of Worship
Austria is predominantly Roman Catholic, but other faiths are well represented in the capital. Sunday mass can be awe-

inspiring, accompanied in most churches by orchestral and choral works.

Anglican: Jauresgasse 17–19, 1030-Wien (tel: 713 15 75).
Evangelist: tel: 292 77 81 for information.
Islamic: Am Hubertusdamm 17–19, 1210-Wien (tel: 270 13 890).
Jewish: Seitenstättengasse 4, 1010-Wien (tel: 531 040).
Lutheran: tel: 51 28 392 for

The nave and high altar under the Stephansdom's Gothic vault

information.
Methodist: tel: 604 53 47 for information.
Mormon: tel: 37 32 57 for information.
Roman Catholic: tel: 515 52 375 for information.

Police

The regular *Polizei* (police) wear

DIRECTORY

green caps and jackets over black trousers, and drive white cars. They are readily distinguishable from the traffic police who wear white caps and, in summer, white jackets. Illegal parkers will have to face up to the blue-jacketed *Politessen* (meter patrol). If you are fined for any reason, you may be asked to pay up there and then. If you need the police in an emergency, dial 133.

Post Office

Post Offices are listed in the yellow pages telephone directory under 'Post'. They are generally open Monday to Friday 08.00–12.00hrs and 14.00–18.00hrs. The central post office and Poste Restante is located at Fleischmarkt 19. For late night and weekend services there are post offices at both main railway stations.
If you need postal information, tel: 83 21 01. Stamps can be purchased over the counter and from vending machines at post offices and tobacconists. Telegraphs may be sent from the central office at Börseplatz 1, post offices and by telephone.

Public Transport

Vienna is served by an excellent public transport system which

The State Opera House

comprises buses, trams, subway (U-Bahn) and commuter (S-Bahn) trains. Maps of the system are available at main stops and the central transport office on Karlsplatz.

A good deal for visitors is the special 24-Stunden-Netzkarte, an inexpensive fixed rate pass covering unlimited rides during a single 24-hour period. To validate the pass, you must stamp it one time only before your first ride in an orange *Entwerter* box, found at stations and on board buses and trams. It is available from tourist information offices, newsstands and transit authority ticket windows. If a group of you is going to be travelling together on the public systems, the 8-Tage-Streifenkarte is a convenient eight-day/multiple user pass. Each of its eight fields is a network pass for one person for one day. When you use this, you need to stamp one field per passenger on the first ride of each day. It is available from the same sources as the 24-hour pass and also from the VOR ticket machines in U-Bahn stations and tobacconists (*Tabak/Trafik*).

You can save one-third of the price of single ride tickets by purchasing them in advance in multiples of four.

Machine-issued tickets bought at the time of travel show the line, date and time of your journey. If you use advance purchase tickets, they will need to be validated from an orange *Entwerter* box. A stamped, single-ride ticket is good for one trip in one direction including transfers.

The Vienna Card

In 1995 The Vienna Card was introduced: a Rover Card for use on all public transport, valid for 72 hours from the time the first trip is taken. Available from Vienna hotels and tourist information offices, it also offers discounts for shops, museums, restaurants and city tours over a four-day period. Discounts include 50 per cent on admission to the Hofburg and reduced price tickets to concerts at Schonbrunn Palace

---

Buses operating in the Inner City are marked A; B denotes surburban services. Night buses (N) depart from Schwedenplatz.

Trams provide an extensive network of 35 routes. Like the buses, they are mostly single-manned, with the word *Schaffnerlos* (without conductor) posted on the rear. If you have a ticket, enter the door marked *Entwerter* and have it stamped; if not, enter via the front and buy your ticket (exact money) from the machine or driver. When a tram does boast a conductor, enter by the rear door to purchase the ticket.

U-Bahn (subway) trains offer an efficient alternative service, connecting many of the main points in town. Tickets may be bought at ticket offices or vending machines. Note that the metropolitan **Stadtbahn** trans-city rail service operates partly underground. **Schnellbahn** rapid-transit suburban trains leave from the Südbahnhof for districts on the outskirts of town. The unit fare applies to all destinations within Vienna; otherwise, fares are standard.

DIRECTORY

Taxis are to be found at ranks in busy city locations may be hailed in the street or dial 313 00; 601 60; 401 00.

Senior Citizens
Senior citizens are offered discounts on travel and entrance fees to museums.

Student and Youth Travel
Students with valid student cards are offered discounted fares in some cases and reductions on museum entrance fees. There is a special youth information desk in Vienna called **Jugund-Info Wien**, at Dr Karl-Renner-Ring/Bellaria Passage, *open*: Monday to Friday 12.00–19.00hrs and Saturdays 10.00–19.00hrs (tel: 526 46 370). Information on ·cheap accommodation, youth hostels, inexpensive places to eat, help and advice is available here. Tickets for events, concerts, etc, can also be bought here at reduced prices. Children under seven travel free on all public transport.
A magazine called *Youth Scene Vienna* is available free from tourist information offices.

Telephones
Public *Fernsprecher* telephones are scattered throughout Vienna. These glass-enclosed booths cannot be missed since they are prominently signed with a black receiver inside a yellow circle. All the booths have multi-lingual instructions, but not all of them are equipped for long distance calls. Cheap rate long distance calls can be made at night or on weekends. Collect calls have to be made from telephone centres, such as the 24-hour centre at the main Post Office, Fleischmarkt 19. You can purchase telephone cards (*Telefonwertkarten*) for use in pay phones. To dial out from Vienna use the following country codes:
Australia: 0061
Canada: 001
Ireland: 00353
New Zealand: 0064
UK: 0044
US: 001
To dial Vienna from abroad the codes are as follows:
from Australia: 00 11 43 1
from Canada: 011 43 1
from Ireland: 16 43 1
from New Zealand: 00 43 1
from UK: 00 43 1
from US: 011 43 1
The code for Vienna from within Austria is : 0222.
If you want the information operator for Austria, dial 1611; for information on Germany dial 1612, Europe dial 1613 and rest of the world dial 1614.
Emergency services and other useful numbers are listed on the first page of the telephone book.

Time
Vienna is on Central European Time: four and a half to 10 hours ahead of Canada; seven to nine hours later than Australia; 11 hours later than New Zealand; one hour later than Greenwich Mean Time in winter, plus another hour during daylight saving in summer; and six hours ahead of New York.

Tipping
Hotels and restaurant bills include a service charge, but it is still usual to leave some small change. Taxi drivers and those who perform a service, such as

hairdressers, will expect 10 to 15 per cent as a tip.

Toilets

Public conveniences are located near main thoroughfares and squares and, of course, cafés have rest room facilities. In some cases, there may be a set charge for use of soap and hand towels (as opposed to a tip), and some toilet doors may have coin slots. If they are not labelled WC or with internationally recognised symbols, they will read *Damen* (Ladies) and *Herren* (Gentlemen).

Tourist Offices

For information before you go, the **Austrian National Tourist Office** is represented in several major cities; or you can write direct to the Vienna Tourist Board. **UK** Austrian National Tourist Office, 30 St George Street, London W1R OAL (tel: (0171) 629 0461).
US 500 Fifth Avenue, New York, NY 10110 (tel: (212) 944 6880); 11601 Wilshire Boulevard, Los Angeles, Ca 90025 (tel: (310) 477 3332); 500 North Michigan Avenue, Chicago, Ill 60611 (tel: (312) 644 8029); 1300 Post Oak Boulevard, Houston, Tx 77056 (tel: (713) 850 9999).
There are no branch offices of the Austrian National Tourist Office in Australia, New Zealand and Canada, but the following are addresses for Honorary Representations:
Australia 36 Carrington Street, Sydney 2000, NSW (tel: 299 3621).
Canada 2 Bloor Street East, Suite 3330, Toronto, Ontario (tel: 967 3381).
New Zealand 76 Symonds Street, Seventh Floor, PO Box

310, Auckland (tel: 734 078).
The **Vienna Tourist Board** is based at Obere Augartenstrasse 40, A-1025 Wien (tel: 21 11 40). Once you have landed, there is a tourist information desk in the Arrivals Hall of Vienna's International Airport (*open*: daily 08.30–22.00hrs or 23.00hrs in season); also at Kärntnerstrasse 38 (*open*: daily 09.00–19.00hrs; tel: 513 88 92). Motorists approaching Vienna from the west can obtain information at the Wien Auhof exit from the A1 Expressway (*open*: daily 08.00–18.00hrs or 22.00hrs in summer); and at the Wien Zentrum exit from the A2 Expressway from southern Austria (*open*: daily 09.00– 19.00hrs in winter; 08.00–22.00hrs in summer).

Tours

If time is short, one of the best ways to catch the highlights of the city is an organised tour.
Gray Line-Cityrama at Börsegasse l/Tiefer Graben 25 (tel: 534 130) offer a terrific range of day and half-day tours in and around Vienna. Classic favourites include the Spanish Riding School, Strauss' Vienna Woods and Mayerling. For a more personal touch, you can arrange your itinerary with a knowledgeable local from **The Vienna Guide Service**, Sommerhaidenweg 124 (tel: 440 30 94); or **Travel Point**, Boltzmanngasse 19 (tel: 319 42 43). Maybe a river cruise would be just the ticket. You will find details at the Tourist Office, or direct from the **DDSG** information counter at Wien-Reichsbrücke dock (*open*: April to October daily 07.30–20.00hrs).

LANGUAGE

Austria's official language is German, but while there is little difference in the way the Austrians and Germans write the language, there is quite a noticeable difference in pronunciation. As with other countries, there are regional differences of accent, and Viennese is the most individualistic of them all. Women may well be addressed as *Gnädige Frau* (Gracious Lady), which may be coupled with *Küss die Hand* (kiss your hand), whether or not the gentleman in question actually makes the action to suit the phrase. It is polite to know at least the basic words of greeting, even though English is the second language in Austria, spoken by numerous Viennese.

Pronunciation

a (short)	as in under
a (long)	as in father
ä (short)	as in bet
ä (long)	as in gate
b	as in bed
d	as in din
e (short)	as in bed or but
e (long)	as in mean or the French word revue
f	as in fog
g	as in get
h	as in hand; ch is pronounced as in Loch or as in huge
i	as in bit; ie is pronounced as in he, and ei as in sight
j	as in jet
k	as in kick
l	as in long
m	as in meet
n	as in no
o (short)	as in not
o (long)	as in hole; oi is pronounced wo as in worry
ö (short)	as in burr
ö (long)	no equivalent in English; purse lips and pronounce short i
p	as in pen
r	as in French r or a rolled English r
s	as in sit
t	as in tea
u (short)	as in put
u (long)	as in woo
ü	follow the same guide as for long o
v	as in vet
w	as in veal
y	as in year
z	as in zebra

Some Phrases

Guten Tag good day
Guten Abend good evening
auf Wiedersehen goodbye
ja yes
nein no
bitte please
danke thank you
gross large
klein small
kalt cold
offen open
geschlossen closed
morgen tomorrow
gestern yesterday
heute today

Probably the biggest difficulty you will encounter on the language front is reading a menu. Few restaurants have them in English, and you will probably need a good pocket dictionary to ensure you enjoy your meal. The main menu headings are:

Suppen soup
Kalte Vorspeisen cold starters and entrées

Fische fish
Schalen und Krustentiere shellfish
Fleisch meat
Geflügel poultry
Wild game
Gemüse vegetables
Süsspeisen or **Mehlspeisen** desserts
Other common menu words are:
Beinfleisch boiled beef

Rostbraten roast beef
Rindfleisch beef
Ente duck
Hendel chicken
Kalbfleisch veal
Schinken ham
Schweinefleisch pork
Erdäpfel or **Kartoffeln** potatoes
Käse cheese
Brot bread
ein Bier a beer
Weisswein white wine

INDEX/ACKNOWLEDGEMENTS

The Automobile Association wishes to thank the following photographers, libraries and associations for their assistance in the preparation of this book.

DAVID NOBLE took all the pictures in this book (© AA PHOTO LIBRARY) except:

AUSTRIAN TOURIST BOARD
20 Vienna Boys' Choir, 32/3 Kaiserappartements, 34 Kaiser's Crown, 35 Kapuzinerkirche, 48 Spanische Reitschule, 64 Dürnstein Castle, 66 Melk.

MARY EVANS PICTURE LIBRARY
10 Maria Theresa, 13 Johann Strauss, 14 Universal Exhibition.

NATURE PHOTOGRAPHERS LTD
72 White stork (P R Sterry), 73 Great reed warbler (K J Carlson), 74 Sand lizard, 77 Apollo butterfly (P R Sterry).

Contributors
For this revision: Copy editor: Claire Watkins
Thanks also to **Carole Chester** for her revision work, and the **ÖAMTC** (Austrian Automobile Club) for checking the Directory section.